*Dedicated to those whose memories
are cherished and celebrated by family
and friends on these pages.*

*There are stars whose radiance is visible on earth even
though they have long been extinct...*

—*Hannah Senesh*

Giving a Voice to Sorrow

Giving a Voice to Sorrow

to Sorrow

*Personal Responses
to Death and Mourning*

STEVE ZEITLIN
AND ILANA HARLOW

A Perigee Book

A Perigee Book
Published by The Berkley Publishing Group
A division of Penguin Putnam Inc.
375 Hudson Street
New York, New York 10014

Copyright © 2001 by Steve Zeitlin and Ilana Harlow
Text design by Tiffany Kukec
Cover design by Wendy Bass
Cover photo of cactus flower from Santiago, Chile/Superstock

First edition: November 2001
Published simultaneously in Canada.

Visit our website at
www.penguinputnam.com

Library of Congress Cataloging-in-Publication Data

Zeitlin, Steven J.
Giving a voice to sorrow : personal responses to death and mourning /
Steve Zeitlin and Ilana Harlow.
p.   cm.
Includes bibliographical references.
ISBN 0-399-52717-6
1. Grief.   2. Bereavement—Psychological aspects.   3. Death—Psychological
aspects.   I. Harlow, Ilana Beth.   II. Title.

BF575.G7 Z45 2001
306.9—dc21

2001016381

PRINTED IN THE UNITED STATES OF AMERICA

10   9   8   7   6   5   4   3   2   1

Give sorrow words; the grief that does not speak
Whispers the o'er-fraught heart, and bids it break.
—William Shakespeare, *Macbeth* IV:III

Contents

Acknowledgments

We would like to thank Jules Harlow, Heather Zacker and Amanda Dargan for their perceptive readings of the manuscript, Robert Butler and Marc Kaminsky, Barbara Kirshenblatt-Gimblett, and Roslyn Bresnick-Perry for sharing their insights and stories with us. Thanks also to friends and colleagues who put us in touch with some of the remarkable individuals in the book: Deborah Kodish, Susan Perlstein, Joe Richmond, Joseph Sciorra, Andrea Sherman, Laura Silver, Joel Sperber, Jack Tchen, Kay Turner, and Lila Zeiger.

ONE

Giving Shape to Sorrow

A Buddhist tale. A wealthy man of the Savatthi country in India married a young girl, Kiságotamí. In time, she gave birth to a son. When the boy grew to the age that he was able to walk by himself, he died. The young girl, in her love for him, carried the dead child clasped to her bosom and went from house to house, asking if anyone would give her some medicine for him. When the neighbors saw this, they said, "Is the girl mad, that she carries about on her breast the dead body of her son?"

In desperation, she visited a holy man and asked him to cure her son. "I can do so," he said. "What I will need is a handful of mustard seed." The girl promised to find some. "But," he continued, "I require some mustard seed taken from a house where no one has died."

"Very good," she said and went to ask for some at the different houses. Yet she could not find a single house that had not suffered loss.

"The living are few, but the dead are many," she was told. One said, "I have lost a son"; another, "I have lost my parents"; another, "I have lost my husband."

At last, not being able to find a house where no one had died, she began to think, "This is a heavy task that I am engaged in. I am not the only one whose son is dead. All over Savatthi children are dying, parents are dying." With these thoughts, she summoned up resolution and left her son's body in the forest.

In this tale, found in different versions around the world, a young woman confronted with unfathomable loss comes to accept the human condition. Through her futile quest for a home that has never known sorrow, she is inducted into a community of mourners; she encounters neighbors who carry on despite devastating losses. She learns that it is indeed possible to endure and that endurance is the way of the world.

The young woman's search evokes stories from her neighbors about the deaths of loved ones. In this way, the bereft mother is in a sense provided with a "grief support group" whose members share stories about their experiences of loss. This book is also a "grief support group" of sorts, a sharing of stories. It presents a variety of creative ways through which people have responded to the imminent loss of their own lives or to the loss of loved ones. *Giving a Voice to Sorrow* explores how we use storytelling, ritual, and commemorative art to cope with death and to celebrate life. It both documents and encourages *outward* expressions of *inner* struggles.

Over the past half century, a number of scholars have sought to chronicle the *inward* processes that individuals go through as they experience old age and death. In 1950, psychoanalyst Erik Erikson wrote that the key issue for people at the end of life is "ego integrity versus despair": acceptance of their own life as they lived it versus despair over not having had time or opportunity to try out alternate paths.

In 1963, psychiatrist Robert Butler introduced the concept of "life review." He suggested that the elderly engage in a mental process of looking back over their lives and evaluating them. He argued that reminiscence, often misinterpreted as a form of senility, can be a creative process through which people make sense of their lives in the face of death. Often they reflect upon past conflicts and are able to achieve resolution, a sense of integration, and serenity before they leave this world.

In 1969, psychiatrist Elisabeth Kübler-Ross suggested that most people, upon being diagnosed with a terminal condition, experience five psychological states—denial, anger, bargaining, depression, and acceptance—as they confront their deaths. Those confronting the deaths of loved ones often experience similar psychological reactions.

This book complements the work of these pioneering psychiatrists by chronicling contemporary *outward* expressions of loss, love, and longing that people craft in response to death. Creativity can help people to transform and even to transcend difficult situations. Many *traditional* responses to death involve the creative impulse through stories, music, art, and rituals connected to funerary rites. In our time, in addition to these traditions and sometimes in lieu of them, it has become increasingly common to find mourners and the terminally ill engaged in personal—and often shared—creative acts. Yet the growing diversity of expressive responses to death cannot be looked at simply as a trend—each is a personal response to a struggle in the consciousness of a bereaved individual.

Artful presentations of our experiences and memories help us to grasp them, and sometimes grapple with them, more concretely. Though art is at a level of abstraction removed from the day-to-day business of life, we often recognize ourselves in it. Ross Abrams, a friend, once related that his young son's favorite story was a retelling of his own day. Ross would begin the storytelling session each evening, "Once there was a little boy named Saul, and he woke up in the morning and had a bowl of Cheerios." Then he would recount the boy's activities throughout the course of the day. The everyday events of the past twelve hours became wonderfully engaging when recast in story form. The effect lies in the transformation of daily life into story—into art. Such artistry moves life toward a transcendent plane. It both connects us to things greater than ourselves and helps us see our own situations with greater clarity.

"One does not possess one's past," wrote existential philosopher Jean Paul Sartre, "as one possesses a thing one can hold in one's hand, inspecting every side of it; in order to possess it, I must bind it to existence by a project." Increasingly, the dying and the bereaved engage in creative personal projects that help them possess their past. Those who no longer walk the earth are dust and spirit. We can only know them through the creations that they leave behind—memory albums, letters, poetry, drawings, music—or through our memories of a shared past with them. Commemorative narratives, rituals, and art that we create from those memories can capture the essence of a person who has died and serve to evoke his or her presence among the living. These artful forms of rememberance have a particular poignancy because the motives behind them—evoking a loved one, recalling a life, shaping sorrow—are so pure.

Undertaker and poet Thomas Lynch of Michigan believes that we have a fundamental obligation to witness our dead. "That's the basic transaction of humanity 'We will get you from this life into the next life, whatever that is or isn't and then we'll remember you.'"

Religious funerary rituals are often about tending to the dead person's eternal soul. *Rituals of remembrance* are about the care and nurturing of a human spirit that dwells among the living in story, memory, family history, and tradition.

CHANGING THE WAY WE DIE

As the baby boom generation moves through the lifecycle, it is transforming every stage of it. As young adults, its members influenced our attitudes toward sex and marriage. In middle age they are changing the way we care for the elderly and the way we die.

A contemporary generation is making personal creativity an increasingly common part of death and dying. Many Americans today do not identify with a single religion but are "cafeteria believers," as Thomas Lynch put it; they "pick and choose" appealing rituals and symbols from religions to which they do not necessarily belong.

Lynch talked with us about the rising trends in cremation in the United States, which he connects to an increasingly secular, increasingly mobile society. He observes that as cremation has become more commonplace in America, there has been a corresponding rise in creative ways of dispersing the ashes. He explained:

In thirty years we've gone from a country that cremates three to four percent of its dead to a country that cremates thirty percent of its dead. This is a radical shift, and it's completely attached to the secularization of the culture. In most of Western religious thought fire is punitive—when you were in trouble with God you burned in hell. For people in Western cultures to burn their dead is not the same as doing it in Eastern cultures where fire is purifying and releasing. This is why in the East they burn, in the West they bury. But in the West, in one generation, we've gone from a culture that buries to a culture that burns.

It's not right or wrong to bury, or right or wrong to burn—it's how we do it. It's not a question of *what* is done but *how* it's done. Our culture doesn't place any ceremonial value in cremation, whereas in Calcutta cremation is public, and it's attended by a lot of symbolic and ritualized behavior. Fire is brought by the first-born child from the home to ignite the fire. But here cremation is often minimalization, disappearance. So people never say, "Please cremate me," they say, "Just cremate me." The emphasis is on the "just" part. Cremation helps keep us mobile—when you cremate someone you end up with ashes, unlike when you bury them. How do we consider those remnants? Are they leftovers? Are they icons? Are they relics? What are they? Everybody gets to decide that for themselves.

It used to be that people would cremate their dead and then put the ashes in a columbarium or put them in a family lot. But now cremation makes the dead mobile. And it makes them divisible. You can't divide a body but you can divide up the ashes. A son will say, "Dad liked to fish in the river; he'd have liked to be scattered there." But Mom says, "Yeah, but I'd like to have Dad buried with me." And the daughter who lives in California says, "Yeah, but what about me?" So she'll take some in a locket, the son will scatter some up where he and his dad fished, and Mom will keep some at home to be buried with her when she dies. Those are creative responses to mortality.

The growing involvement of families in caring for their dead is part of a movement that can be seen in other life-cycle events as well. Lynch continues:

> The men in my generation, the baby boomers, "*refused* to sit out in some waiting room with a handful of cigars. They had to be there. They had to witness it to say, "Breathe, honey, breathe," or whatever. It was of no particular use, but it invested meaning in the whole process and it made them fathers in a way that sitting out in the waiting room would not. The women of my generation were not willing to let their parents die surrounded by machinery and intensive care. They said, "We're going to take them home." I think the hospice movement started with the women in my generation—their refusal to let this huge existential event take place surrounded by machinery. They said, "No. We can do this better. We can take care of the dying better even though we might lose a few days in the process. The humanity will be worth it." They see their obligations to be present, to witness, to take part in, and to do.

Formal religion has often governed our responses toward death, dictating the ways we are buried, the ways we try to comfort the bereaved, and the ways in which we mourn and memorialize loved ones. These traditions tell us how to act and what to say at times when we otherwise might not know what to do or say. They provide comfort.

Sometimes, traditional responses do not satisfy. People who are not affiliated with a religious community often create secular rituals to mark someone's passing. As Dan Silverman commented about the rituals surrounding the death of a teenager in his own community, "These are ceremonies that we've created ourselves. They're not anybody's liturgy or anybody else's ritual. They're expressions of our own spirituality—without the need for somebody else's formalistic rules. It feels much more real to those of us who are not interested in anybody else's ceremony to have created our own."

Even people who are affiliated with a religious community often feel the need for more personal responses in addition to the formal institutional rites. Also, there are some losses that religious institutions or society at large have not formally recognized, and, therefore, have not devised formal ways of mourning for them. Grief over a miscarriage; a stillborn baby; or the death of an ex-spouse, unmarried partner, or extramarital lover have all been defined as instances of "disenfranchised grief," by Lutheran minister and Professor of Gerontology, Kenneth Doka. These losses are sometimes addressed through private, personal rituals.

Folklorist Erika Brady has studied private rituals of grief, including ones enacted by "those whose relationship with the deceased was socially ambiguous, giving them no clearly recognized social role in communal rituals surrounding death." She presents the story of Corinne D., a woman who had been involved with a married man who was separated from his wife. On a number of occasions he had threatened suicide, but she had stopped taking these threats seriously. One night she received a frantic phone call in which he said that he was about to take an overdose of sleeping pills—something he had said many times before. After not hearing from him for two days, she visited his apartment, where she found him dead.

"The pieces of a bone ring she had given him lay next to his hand, having split off his finger as the body swelled. After taking up the pieces she called the police. From that point, the funeral arrangements were in the hands of her lover's estranged wife, leaving Corinne with no defined role to play aside from that of the many mourners who were not members of the immediate family. Privately, she begged the funeral director to place the pieces of the broken ring in the casket with her lover."

The shattered ring symbolized an unsanctioned and troubled love affair, suggests Erika Brady. Its placement in the coffin gave Corinne a secret, physical presence at the funeral. Corinne's act can be understood "as a discreet challenge to those whose official relationship with him allowed them special rights over his body in death but excluded her."

The grief of those affected by the death of unmarried partners or newborn babies often is not validated in our society. Many people attempt to comfort women who have had miscarriages by saying, "You'll have another baby," or "It's for the best. The baby wouldn't have been healthy." These inadequate responses do not acknowledge the reality of loss. In recent years people have been finding ways to validate disenfranchised grief and address it through the creation of new rituals. Today, many hospitals have institutionalized rites that are enacted in response to the death of stillborn and newborn babies, such as dressing the dead babies, giving them to the parents to hold, and taking pictures of them. The parents are thus given memories and mementos of the lives that were never lived.

The current trend in creative response to death has rediscovered some Victorian death customs considered morbid a generation ago. These include the sewing of mourning quilts, made out of clothing of the deceased, and formal photographs of the dead. The hospice movement has helped to revive another death rite from the past—the formal deathbed scene in which the dying assemble their loved ones around them.

Hospice focuses on palliative care, or pain relief, rather than on curing the terminally ill or prolonging their lives. Those in hospice care often die at home amidst friends and family rather than amidst a tangle of tubing from life-support machinery in a hospital. The scholar Philippe Ariès has written about how hospitals transformed dying from a social event to a technological one. Hospice is helping the dying and their loved ones reclaim death as a rite of passage.

In his book *The Last Passage: Recovering a Death of Our Own,* Donald Heinz encourages us to claim our deaths. Death is a great mythological issue which we must confront, writes Heinz. Yet many of us, lacking close-knit communities and traditional religious beliefs, lack the resources to do so. And existing death rituals are inadequate for those who feel alienated by formal religion. For many, the "high drama of death" has been turned into "ritual boredom." At funerals we often sit passively as audience members listening to words; we are not involved as active participants. Heinz suggests that good rituals involve bodies moving and being moved, shaping and being shaped by ritual action. He proposes that we recover the "lost art of dying," recommending that we stage community-based rites of last passage to evoke the drama of death—of exits and entrances, absence and presence, chaos and order. In designing rituals we must ask ourselves, "What about the deceased do we want to remember and celebrate? What homage is to be paid to the sacred? How can the arts help us in this?"

GIVING A VOICE TO SORROW

"Grief is really the other side of the coin of loving," said Thomas Lynch. "It is the tax we pay on our attachments. In a very *real* sense it is the *sign* of our humanity. It's the *sign* of what's best about us."

This book presents contemporary ways that grieving souls have given shape to sorrow. The stories depict ways that individuals and communities have used the arts to accompany their loved ones through the last passage. Each of the personal histories set down in these pages represents a bit of vernacular wisdom and a creativity of everyday life. The narratives are organized according to three forms of creative response: storytelling, ritual, and commemorative art, although we recognize that the categories constantly overlap. Storytelling and the process of creating commemorative art can become rituals, for instance, and rituals often include both commemorative art and stories.

Stories are a way of bringing the departed to life in words. The narrative impulse to tell the life stories of the dead, and thus to conjure up their essence, is a creative act that counters the destructiveness of death. When we put our experiences with the dead into words after they have died, we are creating the memory structures that will contain the kernel of the story for the rest of our lives. "Talking is remembering," writes Roger C. Schank, and telling a story over time often makes it emblematic of a life.

When we don't know what to say, we "do." Ritual actions effect change in the world. They are transforming. Rituals following a death move both the dead and the living from one stage of life to the next, often following the three phases noted by anthropologist Arnold Van Gennep in his book *Les Rites de Passage:* separation, transition, and incorporation. Funerary rites separate the dead from the living, transform them into ancestors, and incorporate them into the hereafter, attempting to secure a safe journey to a permanent resting place. Death rituals separate mourners from the rest of society for a set period of time requiring that they dress and conduct themselves according to their new status and eventually reincorporating them. Rituals also can serve to transform the dead from corpse to spirit and memory. And they can help the living incorporate the departed into their lives.

Commemorative art is a more concrete way to keep loved ones present in our lives. We create gravestones, along with tangible and audible works of art and music that express our sentiments and often convey something about the personality of the deceased. The process of creating such art can almost feel like a ritual. It is a physical enactment of grief.

We give a voice to sorrow in all three of these forms—storytelling, ritual, and commemorative art—and in this book we move from the most ephemeral, stories made of words, to rituals comprised of actions, to commemorative art crafted from the physical world.

With the deaths of those close to us, we mourn ourselves as well. At their funerals and memorials, we rehearse our own lines and scripts. Later, as we face our own deaths, we often engage in a process of life review, a form of storytelling, and create our own memorials. Each section of this book demonstrates not only how we are remembered, but also how we shape our own life stories while we are still alive. Often, as Lisa Lipkin phrased it, the dying are "planning for the past," creating an ending for their own life story. As people confront their death, they sometimes try to form cohesive narratives of their life by writing their life story or telling it to their children. Sometimes, the dying will ask for their ashes to be scattered on a certain mountaintop or a lake, both connecting them permanently to a place they loved and creating a bonding ritual for those charged with the responsibility. Many of the stories, rituals, and artworks presented in this book are collaborations between the living and the dead. They serve as testaments to enduring relationships.

Giving a Voice to Sorrow begins with a single story: The saga of teenager Jesse Shantz and the community of artists and free spirits who, through a series of creative acts, forged an extended family that saw him through his tragic death and devised a series of moving tributes to remember him by. "They don't bring Jesse back to life," says his mother, "but they keep him present in our lives." We begin with Jesse's story because, in the vast outpouring of grief and creative expression that accompanied both his dying and the celebrations of his life that followed, the three forms of responses to death presented in this book come together. His story demonstrates how storytelling, ritual and ceremony, and commemorative art, are interwoven. The stories of the individuals introduced later in the book are not presented in as much detail. Jesse's story illustrates the richness that lies behind each and every life and death.

REMEMBRANCE

We sometimes speak of the desire for immortality. Yet most of us, contemplating our own deaths, are not so concerned with the way we may or may not be recalled in five hundred years on the tongues of strangers. We are most concerned with leaving a mark on the next generation, on our equally mortal children and grandchildren. We desire to have our own lives woven into theirs. When death spirits away a member of society, those who remain must determine ways to maintain their relationships with the departed, to integrate them into their lives. Simple gestures such as a reminiscence or the commemoration of a birthday or anniversary of death provide us not with life everlasting but with what poet William Wordsworth called "intimations of immortality."

"You can keep the things of bronze and stone," writer Damon Runyon is purported to have said on his deathbed. "Just give me one man to remember me once a year." Some cultures put forth the belief that a person is not really dead until the last person who remembers him or her is also gone. For most of us, it is sufficient to know that we will be recalled in living memory—in what anthropologist Margaret Mead called the "human unit of time": "The space between a grandfather's memory of his own childhood and a grandson's knowledge of those memories as he heard about them."

SENSE OF PLACE

We want to be remembered over time. And each of us will be remembered particularly at certain times of the year. We also will be remembered at certain spots that were associated with us in our lives or that become associated with us in our deaths. We even want to die in particular places.

In the city of Benares, India, funeral pyres line the banks of the Ganges River. Benares is the City of Shiva, the great Lord of Death and Destruction, who dances over the city and swoops up souls. Devoted Hindus long to fall into his arms at death. They come to Benares to die with purses of rupees that they have saved for their funeral pyres. After they are cremated, their ashes will be scattered in the Ganges.

In a South Asian neighborhood in Queens, New York, it is possible to buy sealed copper vessels of water from the Ganges. The water is to be sprinkled on the dead who die away from the sacred place to purify them before cremation.

Place matters. It contains our experiences and memories. Sometimes the bodies of Indian Hindus, as well as of members of other immigrant communities, are shipped back to their native land for cremation or burial. The bodies of Jews are sometimes flown to Israel for burial in the Holy Land. Jews buried in the diaspora often have a bag of soil from the land of Israel placed in their coffins. The biblical Joseph, who died in Egypt, requested burial in Canaan, his homeland. The Children of Israel carried Joseph's bones with them as they wandered through the desert for forty years, on their way to the Promised Land.

In a Queens cemetery, an inscription on a Lithuanian gravestone reads, "Rest in peace far from your native land." The depth of association between a person, his birthplace, and his gravesite was expressed in simple eloquence by poet Rupert Brooke, an Englishman who served in and died during the First World War. In his beautiful sonnet, "The Soldier," which envisions his patriotic death, he wrote:

If I should die, think only this of me,
That there's some corner of a foreign field
That is forever England.

Ultimately, the body itself is the place where we live, and dying is about leaving that place. It is the site of experience. It is our home and our coffin. As Bosnian writer Semezdin Mehmedinovic put it, we inhabit "the space of our own mortality."

Often, we think of our cherished rooms and homes as extensions of ourselves—a part of ourselves made of more durable materials that will extend beyond our lifetimes. This is where we often want to find ourselves at the moment of death. Many Americans today want to die at home, surrounded by their lives.

Artist C Bangs talked about moving her father's hospital bed into his study in the months before he died. "He felt very good in his study," she told us, "because he was surrounded by his books, by the awards he had received, by his work, and who he was. My mother and father had pictures on the wall in the bedroom, too, but it was just a bedroom. In the study, he felt grounded—he was surrounded by his life. Every time he went into the hospital, there was a dramatic decline and then he would come back home to his study and he would spring back."

Many people establish a place where, they believe, the spirit of the dead reside, even if their physical remains are elsewhere. When Barbara Kirshenblatt-Gimblett's sister died, her nephew sensed the presence of his mother, who had been a piano teacher, in the house.

"Where is she?" asked the grown-ups.

"On Middle C," he said.

When a person no longer inhabits the body, a place must be found for the remains. The deceased and their loved ones sometimes collaborate on this creative choice; in order to decide, both need to determine what the life in question stood for, what characteristics defined that life, and match them with an appropriate place in the environment. Burial in an appropriate site is about a family or community putting individuals into context and thus giving them meaning, noted Peggy King-Jorde. Edna Anderson told us, "My husband, Dole, traveled all his life, so we thought it was most appropriate to scatter his ashes at sea—because the sea touches all the places he lived and loved." Jesse Shantz's mother was inclined to scatter his ashes over all the far-flung beaches that he loved, but Jesse told her that he wanted to be buried close by, "so people could visit."

Many of us want to know we will be visited when we are dead; and those who love us want a place where they can come visit. When someone is lost at sea, or when a plane falls into the ocean, mourners bring flowers to the seaside; they want to get as close as possible. They approach the place where it seems the souls of the dead must hover. Yet this mourning at a distance at a vaguely appointed spot often fails to satisfy. In Melville's *Moby Dick*, Ishmael enters a seaside chapel in which there are markers for those lost at sea, "beings who have placelessly perished without a grave." He appreciates that the desolation of mourners for these dead is much greater than mourners "whose dead lie buried beneath the green grass" who can say, "here, here lies my beloved."

The families of those who perished in the Holocaust and other atrocities do not know where the bodies of their loved ones lie.

Their situation provides a striking reminder about the importance of a gravesite both for the dead and for the living. For Toby Blum-Dobkin's father, Boris Blum, a name on a tombstone was not something to take for granted. His grandparents were killed in a pogrom, a violent, anti-Semitic attack in the Ukraine. His parents perished in the Holocaust. A survivor of the Warsaw ghetto and the death camps of Majdanek, Buchenwald, and Dachau, Boris had witnessed piles of corpses taken to the crematoria and burned. Once, a doctor conducting a medical history asked him to name any fatal diseases that had taken members of his family. He had no answer because no family member in living memory had died a natural death. If he were given a funeral and a tombstone, Boris would be the first member of his family in three generations to have them. As he put it, it would be "like being published."

Boris Blum died suddenly of a heart attack on Passover in 1985. His family worked hard designing the tombstone that meant so much to him, inscribing it not only with the dates of his birth and death, but the date of his liberation from the camps. On it, they placed a memorial to all family members who had been killed and who had no tombstone. At the top of the stone are words taken from the Talmud, an ancient Jewish text, which are appropriate for a printer and a printer's son: "The scroll burns, but the letters rise."

THE ENACTMENT OF GRIEF

When Steve looks back at his mother's death, he remembers the last day she was conscious. She was in intensive care and visiting hours were over. As he was leaving, he said to her, "I love you,

Mom." She answered. "I love you, too, and I love my whole family." In happier times, saying "I love you" signified a willingness to do anything for one another. When he told his mother "I love you" as she was dying, the words had a different meaning. He felt that what he was saying to her was, "I can only love you, Mom, I can't cure you, I can't really do anything for you right now except tell you how much I love you." It was a vulnerable love—filled with the pathos of the human condition.

Before her mother's death, Maida Owens, of Baton Rouge, Louisiana, cared for her for almost three years. Maida, too, recognized that there was nothing she could *do*. She could only *be*. Her mother was weakened on one side of her body as the result of a stroke. "I'm very much a doer like my mother was," Maida told us. "I like projects, I like organizing. So I'm very much my mother's daughter. When you strip away the ability to do things, what's left? You just have to *be*. Sometimes I would take her out for a drive and we would go for thirty minutes in complete silence. It didn't come naturally, but the two of us had to learn how to just be."

After her mother died, Maida could become a doer once again. She says that when she visits her mother's grave, "It's really important for me to bring something to leave there. She was a chocoholic, so the obvious thing is chocolate. Chocolate was what made her happy right up until the very end. So, I'll sometimes buy a candy bar— you know she had certain ones that she liked—and I'll put a ribbon on it, a bow, just to be able to leave it there. To me, it's like putting my grieving into action. I get to go pick out something and physically take it somewhere and put it somewhere. The physicalness of it is part of the release."

The stories, rituals, and commemorative art chronicled here are examples of the kinds of creative enactments of grief that can give us some measure of control over situations that have savagely rent the fabric of our lives.

This book is comprised primarily of personal interviews. Individuals who have suffered or witnessed great loss relate personal responses to death and mourning in their own words. They transport us to *inward* places where love, sadness, and creativity meet; places where they forged responses to death whose *outward* expression enabled them, their friends, or their family to endure devastating loss.

Each of us must find our own pathway through grief. In this life, there are no happy endings. This book serves to map the paths others have walked. It is never easy. As one man put it, the only useful advice anyone ever gave him about coping with his wife's death was this: "Put your right foot in front of your left foot, then your left foot in front of your right foot, and continue moving forward until you return to the world of the living." The wounds never heal completely. "People who blithely say things will get better over time have never been here," remarked Glen McDonald who lost his teenage son Chad in a shooting accident. "Things never get better. They get a little less immediate."

We hope that the stories in this book might serve as inspiration to those who are just beginning similar journeys. This is not a "how-to" book for dying and mourning. There is no "right way" to die. There is no one way to mourn, no single way to express one's sorrow. Eventually, the emotional responses of sadness, horror, and anger over death make way for creative responses as people struggle to endure despite their grief. As we sought out creative responses to death, outward expressions of inner lives, we were privileged to gain glimpses into the hearts, minds, and souls of some remarkable individuals. We, like the young mother in the tale that opened this chapter, have visited many houses that have known sorrow. In this book, we share some of the voices that have saddened and inspired us. Yet, like the residents of Savatthi, we can provide no mustard seed.

TWO

Jesse's Story

—*Told by Kristen Shantz, Dennis Cunningham,
and the Wellfleet Community*

Jesse Shantz's death at the age of nineteen after a five-year battle with cancer galvanized his community of family and friends to create stories, rituals, and commemorative art to mourn his death and celebrate his life.

When the Pilgrims, escaping religious persecution, approached the New World on the *Mayflower* in 1620, they landed first on Cape Cod, the spit of land that juts into the Atlantic to form Massachusetts Bay. A few weeks later, unable to find fresh water, most crossed over to the mainland, where they founded Plymouth Colony. But they were back a few years later.

When a group of rebellious souls in the late 1960s and early '70s, escaping the confines of organized religion, parental control, and what they considered repressive society, drifted up to Wellfleet to wile away stray summers on the outer part of the Cape, they, too, fell in love with the duned beaches and nestled ponds and could not stay away for long.

Many of these modern-day pilgrims were rebels and hippies who followed their bliss out to a place by the sea. They eventually married one another, and some got divorced and married their friends' wives and husbands, but they all remained friends. At times, the mothers even nursed one another's children if the situation called for it. And they all closed like family around Kristen Shantz and Dennis Cunningham when their son Jesse was diagnosed with cancer, through his death in 1997, and until this day.

Jesse was one of the "Fleetians," as the Wellfleet teenagers referred to themselves, tall and lanky, with expressive hands and such beautiful features that it is difficult to stop staring at the photographs of him as both child and teenager. From the age of fourteen, when he was first diagnosed, until his death at the age of nineteen, Jesse juggled what it meant to be a teenager with cancer and his life as a carefree Fleetian, listening to Bob Marley, surfing, and hanging out down by the ponds.

The Pilgrims sailed into the Bay on the sturdy wooden ship of traditional religion. Kristen, Dennis, and the Wellfleet Community, confronting Jesse's death, had to construct their own ship as they sailed, using memory, ritual, stories, and art to carry them through.

The artistic expression that emerged from Jesse's life and death garners its beauty from the grief and passion of this beautiful teenager, his family, and his friends. And his laughter, too.

Jesse's laugh still hangs in the air at Wellfleet. It still comforts and consoles. People smile to themselves when they think about him. Kristen's friend Paul said, "Every time I drive by the graveyard—every time—I hear Jess laugh one of his great belly laughs. It keeps it light for me. It keeps me right in the moment."

Certain lines and expressions that he used are recalled fondly in stories. Kristen's friend Sharyn remembers, "I came over here to pick up my son Caleb. Suddenly, his brothers and a bunch of other kids piled into the back of my pickup truck. As I zoomed out of Kristen's driveway I hit a tree. All the kids jump out—they're looking at it and Jesse comes running up to the tree. And even now, after his death, I can still hear his voice say, 'Oh my God, Sharyn, don't even look!' "

Through most of his teenage years, Jesse knew he was dying. Often fatigued, he became frustrated at having to go to high school. "It didn't make a whole lot of sense to him," Kristen said, "to wrestle with these really big issues in his head and at the same time have to study for a history test. So he wanted to try home schooling. Starting in his junior year he worked his magic on us." Jesse, his parents, and the principal worked out a program for independent study for Jesse beginning in the eleventh grade. One of his first independent-study projects was at the Center for Coastal Studies. He spent the following summer on whale boats, recording data about the sea creatures.

Jesse loved to travel and kept a push-pin map on his wall of places he'd been. And he argued with Kristen and Dennis that, since he was going to die anyway, he should get all the money they had saved for college and use it to travel around the world. Although his parents did not give in to him completely, they did help him arrange a number of far-flung jaunts. When he was seventeen he went scuba diving in the Red Sea, where he met and romanced a girl named Becky. The family album displays a wonderful photo of the two of them beneath the water. In his travels, the world became his oyster. It was, as his mother put it, "an explosion of new experience—it was sleeping out on the desert with Bedouins, exploring what was beneath the surface of the Red Sea, and discovering romance."

He also took a sleeper car from Boston to Seattle, interacting with people who did not know he had cancer. As Kristen pointed out, "He had to cope with a deadly disease and, on top of that, one that disfigured him. As a teenager, if you look different you want to look different because it's your own choice, not because your hair is falling out. In his travels, he was able to try himself out on the world."

A few days before Jesse died, his friend Lee Kenny recalls him thumbing through a travel magazine. "At that point he must have known how close to death he was," she remembers, "whether it was going to be chemo that would kill him or not doing the chemo that would kill him. But he just sat in his bed, reading through this catalogue of trips that, in the back of his mind, he must have known he wasn't going to go on. But he didn't close the catalogue, he just kept looking at it and talking about the pros and cons of each trip—why you would go on this one but why you wouldn't go on that one." Lee, who returned from Scotland a week before Jesse died, would get under the covers with him, where they would chat, watch movies, or simply cry together. "He just took everything for exactly what it was," she said. "He wasn't at all bitter about any of it."

As we listened to Jesse's story unfold in the words of his family and friends, we thought—and they thought—they were chronicling his life. But, of course, what they told were *stories, representations* of a life. Once we die, our lives are recalled in memory by those who loved us, not by objective observers. The facts of our lives are colored by the need of family and friends to create a coherent, meaningful, and memorable life story.

For Dennis and Kristen these stories and memories rearrange reality so that the world becomes bearable. "It's not to keep a person alive," Kristen said, "it's about keeping a person present—it's not about living in the past, it's about honoring your past—because it makes us all who we are. It's invaluable that I can bring up Jesse's name to anybody and nobody ever thinks, 'Oh, we don't talk about that anymore.' "

Yet the power of all the stories and rituals is limited. "Nothing saves you," a family friend, Kathy Connors, exclaimed. "I think Kristen still thinks about Jesse every day of her life. I know she does. As a parent you can see that. This helps, this helps, but nothing saves you—nothing."

Kristen, even with her short, cropped head of hair, is every bit as beautiful as when she was the rebellious college graduate with flowing waist-length hair who moved to Wellfleet; she is still tall and strong, and rarely pities herself. "I can't change the past. I could feel sorry for myself, and I probably would feel sorry for myself if I were the only person in the world to whom something like this happened, because I would feel picked on. I'm not. Dennis and I went to a support group with eight other parents who had lost their kids. I could have sat there, which I certainly did, and thought, 'Ahh, your kid lived till he was forty—what I would have given for another year, six months, days. Oh, you're so lucky.' Well, they didn't feel lucky. You don't have to look far to see you're not alone."

The tombstones that fill the Wellfleet cemetery go back to the late 1600s. Dennis recalls wandering through this cemetery where his son's ashes are buried. He saw an inscription on an old gravestone that marked the passing of a father and four sons who shared a single date of death. In Wellfleet, he realized that this must have signified a fishing accident. Dennis tried to use that gravestone inscription to put the weight of his own grief in perspective. On one day, a woman lost five of her loved ones. But the pain of others couldn't take away his own. As a friend put it, "Your grief is your grief."

We first learned about Jesse's story from a co-worker who summers occasionally on the Cape. We heard about the "cahuna," the memorial marker the community had raised on the dunes. We were expecting to speak with Jesse's parents for a few hours. As it turned out, we spent two days in Wellfleet and recorded more than ten hours of interviews not only from family but from friends. Many times, for minutes at a time, the tape recorder chronicled only sobs. When we were leaving, family friend Lee Kenny, who held Jesse's hand as he died, wept once again. "There's always crying to be done," she said. "It's never over."

Like the winter of 1620, in which half of the Pilgrims died, Jesse's death, precisely on the Winter Solstice in 1997, was a dark time, a winter whose icy chill would never fully thaw. Though they had few religious beliefs, the former hippies and rebels of Wellfleet found a way to forge some spiritual solace out of the tragedy in their hearts, channeling an enormous outpouring of love and sadness into creative expressions of grief. Like the hero of John Bunyan's seventeenth-century allegory, *Pilgrim's Progress*, they crossed, together, the River of Death. These sorrowful memories mark, for each of them, a pilgrim's progress—the personal, stalwart journeys of a mother and father and the community who loved their son.

"Jesse, We Will Not Rush Grief"
—*Told by Kristen Shantz, Dennis Cunningham,*
and the Wellfleet Community

LOSS OF A TWIN

In 1978, Kristen Shantz gave birth to twin boys, Jesse and Quechua. Quechua died of Sudden Infant Death Syndrome, leaving Jesse as an only child. Kristen and her newfound community of cohorts in Wellfleet did little to commemorate the loss of the baby. Though they did scatter the ashes, the grief went largely unrecognized, unmarked. The unsatisfying lack of ritual taught Kristen not to make the same mistake when Jesse died at the age of nineteen from a rare form of t-cell lymphoma, sometimes called slack skin disease. Kristen recounts:

The cribs were right next to my side of the bed because I was nursing. And in the middle of the night there was a sound, almost an animal-like sound. I can still hear it, but I'm not sure how to describe it. I woke up out of a deep sleep and just scooped Jesse up and brought him to bed with me.

The next morning I remember opening my eyes. The room was very, very still, which with twin babies is quite remarkable. I snuck out of bed and thought, "Oooo, let me just go and sit in the other room for a minute for some peace and quiet." I got up and walked by both of their cribs. But in sneaking out I never looked in the other crib. I went and sat in the rocking chair, relishing a quiet moment—and all of a sudden it hit me, "Oh my God, one of the babies is dead!" I realized the stillness wasn't the quiet of no crying. It was the stillness of death. I ran into the room and screamed.

mourning is something you learn

People came over right away. The police came over and the local doctor and the coroner, and luckily they just did everything right there. We scattered the baby's ashes at the beach. I really didn't know what to do. Death was not a part of my or any of our friends' childhoods. We didn't remember death as having rituals and ceremonies around it. I really didn't know what to do, and neither did anyone else.

Years later when I was going to grief counseling after my mother and father died, a counselor asked me, "Have you ever grieved for your child?" And a lightbulb went off in my head. I actually asked my friend Ann Suggs later that day, "Do you know why we didn't mourn?" And she said, "Because none of us knew what to do. It was new to all of us. One of our babies had died."

We learned a lot without even knowing it. And, in the years that followed, my work in health care with AIDS patients also taught me. I was inspired by the ways the patients and their friends and families found to express their grief and celebrate their lives.

THE PERFECT SUMMER

Lee Kenny, neighbor and friend, played the role of older sister not only for her brother Eben, but for the "three musketeers": Eben, Jesse, and Dan. Lee recalls the one perfect summer when two tents were put up in the yard at the Shantz home. Perhaps this perfect time before everything began to go wrong marks the beginning of the tale. As Lee told it:

We must have been ten, eleven, twelve—middle-school age. It was the last summer of nothing. No drugs, no sex, no alcohol, no cancer—just talking, telling dumb stories. There was a full moon every single night, and shooting stars every single night. And the water was always warm. I know it's not true; it's just in my memory. But it seems we had a beach party every night, and every night it was a full moon and low tide and you could swim and there was phosphorescence in the water. And there was no sex, drugs, or cancer. It was all still perfect.

When we arrived at Kristen and Dennis's home, Jesse's friend Dan Jaffe was waiting for us as well. Although we were asking about the commemorations that followed Jesse's death, Dan and Kristen also wanted to recount the good times. He painted a picture of ten or eleven kids lined up along the beach, running with their boards toward the water and "catching air" as the boogie boards skimmed off the waves. Kristen added that when Jesse was that age, he developed an odd mark on his abdomen, which she initially dismissed as a rash caused by the boogie boards. It turned out to be the first sign of cancer.

SHAVING HEADS

Stack Kenny and Ellen LeBow, an artist, both migrated to Wellfleet from New Rochelle, New York. Joe Tucker, a self-described 240-pound African-American who was a high school friend of both Stack and Ellen, visited often and enjoyed being one of the men in Jesse's life. Jesse loved Joe and his son Noah. They came to visit when they heard that Jesse was starting chemotherapy. One day Joe, Noah, and Jesse improvised a unified response to the effects of the treatment. "It was a thing of the moment. You couldn't not do it," Noah told us. "We were full of hope back then," said Joe.

Kristen remembers:

It just happened to be the time when Jesse's hair was coming out in tufts. So, we went over to Paul and Anne's and we had a head-shaving party. Paul, Joe, Noah, Dennis, and I all shaved Jesse's head. Then Noah wanted his head shaved, too. It was quite amazing, actually, to be around all those bald heads.

Eben and Justin, two other buddies of Jesse's also shaved their heads without any fanfare, in total solidarity for their pal. They never said anything, they just did it.

JESSE'S TREES

The garden that surrounds her house has kept Kristen connected to Jesse and to hope.

As a parent, when you are dealing with such a severe illness of your child and your world is collapsing, there are little touchstones and things that can mean a lot. In the Spring I would step out and look at the trees outside my front door, because these were trees that Jesse gave me for Mother's Day. There was also a rhododendron in the woods behind our house that he gave me for my birthday. You may think they're just plants, but they're not. They are things I can touch. That cherry tree gives me great comfort. When it was full of blossoms in the Spring, I would look at it and somehow think everything was going to be okay, at least for a little while. The tree has provided huge solace for me, both when Jess was alive and since his death. For me, being outside and working in the yard with the plants and watching them grow and change with the cycle of the seasons—all of that helps me go on and allows me to see the continuity in things.

THE SAUNA

The process of remembering Jesse began while he was still living. Kristen had an inspired idea: Jesse should build a sauna as part of his independent study. With his father, Jesse constructed a piece of wooden wizardry that continues to transform grief, and now memory, into a positive, cleansing, healthy, and life-affirming experience. Kristen describes her brainstorm:

The way it happened is that Dennis and I were talking to Jesse about his independent study, and it was one of those "ahas." It popped into my head, and I insisted that it become one of his school projects. Of course he was resistant. And I wouldn't say Dennis was resistant, but he wasn't too sure about it. But the more we talked about it, the more both of them began to like the idea.

I was a little fearful that Jesse was leaving school, and I wasn't sure what he was going to do about college, and I wanted him to learn a practical skill. I figured if he learned how to build a sauna, he would have some practical ability. But aside from developing a skill, I wanted what has actually happened—I wanted to be able to go in there and take a sauna and know that he touched absolutely every part of it. Of course I didn't say to Jess, "When you're gone I'm going to want to go into the sauna because of the whole ritual of the sweating and the purifying and the warmth—that wonderful gift—I want that." I know I didn't explain that to him. I know I did talk about how much it would mean to me to be able have that there forever, as well as the practicality of him learning a skill. I still have the research report he wrote on the Finnish sauna bath. Dennis helped him with lumber lists and had him figure out and draw up the designs.

What was so wonderful was the process of building it with Dennis. This was so precious. I have a photograph that shows Jesse working on it, and you can see his beautiful hands holding one of the beams. When the project started, he was just coming off of a chemo treatment that seemed to have gone well. He wasn't in one of his illness cycles. Yet I knew in my heart that working on the sauna was invaluable, regardless of the outcome. It couldn't go wrong. I knew very instinctively, which is a lot of what I went by at that time.

The Fall that he died, he would be downstairs watching television, and Maria and Ann and I would often go in and take a sauna, and we'd come back and say, "Oh my God, it was so wonderful, we love it so much." And he loved that we loved it. He recognized the importance of his handiwork.

From Dennis's perspective:

Building the sauna was a father-and-son thing. Jesse really did learn a considerable amount about construction. He wasn't able to finish it. We did the framing and the outside together, but he was pretty weak by the end. We finished it the Fall before he died.

It's just amazing to use the sauna in the winter, to come out here and fire it up. You fire up the woodstove, and it takes about a half hour to get it up to temperature—anywhere between one hundred and forty and one hundred and eighty is pretty nice. Then just spray a little water on those rocks and get a teeny bit of steam.

I try to use the sauna in a spiritual way. I think of it as a cleansing, and every time I use it I think of Jesse because I have such great memories of being out here in the Fall and cutting wood. Banging nails with your kid—there's just something about it.

I understand now why Kristen wanted it done as a memorial. It's an active thing. It's something that you *do* rather than something that you just go to or remember. There's a ritual to starting the fire. I love to start the fire and come out here and watch the smoke start to come out of the chimney. That white smoke drifts through the woods, and the smell of it is really wonderful—beautiful on a cold day.

THE BIRTHDAY PRESENT

With time so precious, Kristen was planning for the past. She actively tried to create the memories she would need to remember. Virginia Woolf wrote about "moments of being," those times when life becomes so concentrated that an individual moment seems to exist forever and thus can be readily recalled.

One day, in the summer before Jess died, I had to take him for a medical test. It was on my birthday. It was scheduled for very early in the morning, and he had to go to Plymouth, which was an hour away. And he had to drink what's called contrast for the MRI—it's awful. So, it was pretty rough. And when he got through with the test, he said to me, "I'm sorry, I didn't buy you a present."

And I said, "Well that's okay, don't even worry about it." But then I had an idea. I said to him, "You know, there still is a present you can give me."

He said, "Oh? What?"

And I said, "I'd like you to spend the day with me." Time was precious at this point, and that meant a lot to me.

So, we came back to the house and got lunch, and I said, "You get to pick where we go." He took me to one of the secret spots in Truro, the next town over. We sat up on the highest dune, which is even higher than the dunes at Whitecrest, and ate our sandwiches and walked down the beach. It was an overcast day, and the sun was in and out. It was not quite a swimming day, but I encouraged him to take his shirt off. At this point his skin was hard. The elasticity was gone, so his body was reddish and purplish, and he was very self-conscious about it. But it never looked horrible to me. He was my son. He took his shirt off and was a little uptight at first. We started walking, and I just started talking about other things, and he really got to relax. And I could just see him start to relish feeling the air on his body and being on the beach and able to take his shirt off.

We climbed back up the dune and were walking through the woods to get to the car where we came across a little pond. I don't really know where it was even though I kind of know all the ponds in the area. And we both said, "Let's go for a swim," and for the first time in years, he took his pants and shirt off to go swimming. He just had his boxers on. And he dove into that pond with such a great abandon.

This was one of the best gifts I've ever gotten on my birthday—

just to be able to have that time and be able to watch him be just a little bit more like everybody else—and to share that moment with each other.

ASCENSION

When Jesse's friends went off to college he was often depressed and would retreat to the basement. Kristen's good friend Anne recalls:

He just hung out down on the futon, which was kind of dark, and wore sweats. It took me a while to realize he had a hooded sweatshirt on. I could see he was really lonely.

Then he did this amazing thing. He stopped hanging out in the basement, and he started hanging out up here in the living room. The change was just remarkable. As he was getting sicker and closer to dying, he brought all this light up into the whole house. He spent time on the couch with people coming in and out. Whenever someone came in, he'd always kind of light up and say "hi" and visit for a little while. And really, the house just got brighter and brighter and more and more comforting as more and more people came to see him and to spend time with Kristen and Dennis. The three of them really let that happen, which I think was so amazing because it was really terrifying. I think it would have been almost more instinctual to just shut the doors for protection. Instead, Kristen and Dennis knew, and Jesse knew, that what needed to happen then was for everyone to come in and really be a part of what was going on for him and what was going on for all of us.

Kristin finishes the story:

Paul and Ann were over here all the time, and so were Maria and Kevin. They played backgammon—the sound of those backgammon chips is such a memorable sound to me—and they would laugh and have contests. It was quite wonderful.

And then I remember Jesse asking if he could sleep upstairs. We have a ceiling fan in our bedroom, and he was feeling hot. So we said sure, "Take our bed." We brought the television and VCR up there. He was so grateful for it—"Really? Awesome!"

He was grateful right up to his dying. He was grateful for everything we were doing for him. I actually remember him saying, "Thank you for my life." His last week he told me that he had had a good life—and he really appreciated all of it.

We moved upstairs with him. And at one point he said to me, "I think I'm dying. And I think maybe a lot of people are going to miss me."

"Well," I said to him, "I can't speak for other people, but let me tell you how I feel . . ."

At night I woke instantly to his voice, and I remember he would call and say, "Mom? Mom?" I would say, "Yeah." He would say, "I'm just checkin'." And we would say, "I love you," to each other. It was just this sort of easy, sweet thing. And it happened the last few nights in the hospital too.

In retrospect, I realize that he was slowly moving upward through the house. And I think it was symbolic of his acceptance and profound understanding that he was dying.

Literary critics often assign symbolic meanings to poems and novels that the author may, or may not, have intended. Similarly, mourners attribute motives and significance to the actions of their loved ones that may not have been intended. Or perhaps, unconsciously, they were. It is impossible to know if Jesse was aware of this symbolic ascension from the basement to the living room to the bedroom in his final days. But this story suggests that the stories told about Jesse after his death are a subtle collaboration between Jesse and those who remember him.

THE LAST DAY

Many families tell the story of a child's birth as a ritual on the child's birthday. The story of a person's death has a similar import. A lifetime has a number of defining moments, and the moment of death is likely to be among them. Some of the last words and actions recalled in the story of a person's death may be intentional ones, like Jesse's humorous remarks. Other details of a person's last hours may be biological, but still are assigned meaning, like Jesse's coloring or "glow" when he was dying. Kristen recalls a moment from Jesse's last day:

I remember, on his last day, we were massaging Jesse and rubbing him, and at one point his body—and part of it was his jaundice—seemed to really take on a glow. It might sound a little wacky, but there was a peacefulness about him. And I was massaging him. I felt like I was drinking him in, and I said, "My God, Jesse your arms are so long." It was as if he was growing larger than life. He just had this glow and this benevolent aura or feeling about him, and his eyes are closing and he looks up and he says, "Well, you know what they say about people with long arms?"

And we all whisper, "What?"—Oh you at the doorway to the beyond.

He says, "They have to wear long shirts."
It was sweet. It was pretty sweet.

Kristen and Dennis's close friend, Ellen LeBow recalls a detail from Jesse's death,

Jesse's hands were something we watched all the time in the hospital—because his hands were very long and graceful and attenuated on these arms. On the night he died, his hands were making the most beautiful gestures. It was like watching a fire.

THE CAHUNA

The fire in Jesse's hands as he died and the glow in his face inspired his close friend Dan Jaffe to create, along with a number of members of their community, a fiery yellow sun carved from a locust tree and planted on a fifty-foot dune on Whitecrest beach, visible to surfers on the pounding waves below. Dan tells the story.

I was actually in Lake Tahoe when I got a call from Maria, one of the neighbors, who told me that Jesse might not make it through the night. I got on the next possible flight back. I was met at the airport in Boston by Big Danny and Lee. I walked off the plane and they said he had passed away. It blew me away. I couldn't believe it.

I'll never, ever forget walking into that hospital room after Jesse had died. He was glowing. I walked in there and all the lights were off. All the light in the room was coming from him. He was lying in the bed almost as if he was on a throne, and people were gathered around. He was like a king. He was bright, bright yellow—pure gold.

So I got to sit with him for twenty minutes and just hold his hand and be there with him for a little while. And for the next few days this image was burned into my head—that's what I'd see when I closed my eyes—an image of the sun over the dune at Whitecrest, our favorite beach. I knew I had to build this totem, this cahuna, and set it out over the dune so that surfers could see it from the sea. I sometimes think Jesse channeled the image into my brain.

Dan needed to leave for California in a few days, and the adult community, reeling from the pain of Jesse's death, tried to dissuade him from such an ambitious endeavor. "He wanted to make this big totem," said family friend Dan Silverman. "I mean we could barely find our way out of a chair and here is Dan with this vision. We all lovingly gave him permission not to do it. The intent was wonderful, but it was all right and perfectly understandable if he couldn't get it done. He did get it done—and watching it happen for me was almost musical."

"It was so impressive and almost gentle the way this thing happened," Kristen said, "It was like—wwwwwwwww—a breeze that blew through that just kind of cleared the way for Dan to do it. There was nothing frantic about it." Family friend Chuck Cole helped Dan cut down the tree from the same grove of locust trees that the sauna in Kristen's backyard sits on. Dan Silverman's wife, Janis, helped Dan Jaffe glue three pieces of locust together to form a large wooden square. Family friend and artist Ellen LeBow helped cut out the pattern for the sun, and Dan used a bandsaw to cut out the shape of the sun. Dan Silverman helped notch the tree trunk. Eben and Dan went out to the beach to scout out a spot and dug a six-foot hole for the totem. The next morning at the break of day, the whole community hoisted it on their shoulders and carried it out to Whitecrest. They triumphantly raised it high, looking a bit like the soldiers who hoisted the flag at Iwo Jima. Then they shared muffins and coffee at sunrise.

The "cahuna" became an impromptu shrine. Shells and stones and feathers were left on the sand around it. Eben made a wooden sign on the totem that said, "This sun represents our love for Jesse Shantz." He put Dennis and Kristen's phone number on it and wrote, "Please call this number before removing." Kristen knew that mounting permanent artwork on a national seashore would require an act of Congress. She considered petitioning Congress, but opted instead for the sign. The Park Rangers called a few months later, and members of the community drove to the dune and brought the totem to Kristen and Dennis' backyard—but not before others had benefited from the "cahuna's" power in unexpected ways. Kristen explains:

Jesse's dental hygienist told me this story after Jesse died. She and her husband were trying to adopt a child from overseas and were running into all kinds of setbacks. She was at the end of her rope, and she went out to the beach at a time the cahuna was still up. She was beside herself in tears. So, she went out to the totem and talked to Jesse and asked him to help her. The next day, they received a call that there was, indeed, a baby for them to adopt. Her husband left immediately for China. She told me that about a year afterward.

SHOCK

Kristen recalls the moment when Jesse's best friend Dan walked into the hospital shortly after Jesse died. "Dan and I happened to be on opposite sides of Jesse's bed. We embraced for twenty minutes across the bed. We just cried and wailed." Dan's mother, Sheryl Jaffe, a local artist, later mounted an exhibit about grief and loss. She captured this moment in an installation called "Unconsolable Loss."

For the first days after Jesse died, Kristen and Dan still sensed his presence.

"When I came back to Kristen's house right after he died," Dan said, "I could actually hear him—'cause I actually stayed in his bed a couple of days after he died. The next couple of nights he was still here—do you know what I mean? Like I would turn the corner, and I could hear his little whisper or his laugh upstairs. That's gone now."

The actions immediately following a death can be, as Kristen recalls, compulsively ritualistic.

When Jesse first died I felt like an animal. When I returned to the house after his death, I found myself driven to go into every single room and into every single closet. I couldn't not do it. I remember thinking, "What's happening to me?" I was simply making sure he wasn't here—or hiding.

Every second with Jess is frozen in my psyche, from the time he was diagnosed, to his death, to leaving the room where his body lay. I can pull up the smell or the texture of his skin, because I knew that every moment was precious with him. I even have some clothes of

Jesse's that I keep in a baggie, because I can open the bag up and smell the clothes and I can smell him. Some of these things I don't even share with Dennis.

VISITING

Jesse died on December 21, 1997. The official service marking his death was on January 3, 1998, and the burial was on January 10. On some days, the house would be crowded with people; other times there would be just two or three people. Sometimes, as Stack put it, "You wouldn't talk about Jesse, and sometimes it was so intense that that's all we talked about." As John Connors put it, "In this community, everybody seems to have the capacity to wear their heart on their sleeve."

There were moments of great humor. John Connors, a seemingly gruff but hilarious neighbor and friend whose sense of humor Jesse adored, had made hating the family dog, Luna, a longstanding joke. Dennis approached him during those days following Jesse's death to tell him that Jesse had willed the dog to him. "Jesse left you Luna," Dennis said.

"I'll get my barbecue started," John quipped.

On the days before the service, the beautiful mahogany box made by Dan Silverman and Dan Jaffe that held Jesse's ashes was set up on a low coffee table. A ritual developed. Friends began rubbing the box when they came into the house. Stack Kenny commented, "I think what's wonderful is that nobody said, 'Okay, what we're going to do is put the box on the table and rub it.' Nobody said anything like that. It just evolved."

Kristen and Bill Clark, a Unitarian minister who is close to the family, saw a need to get the kids involved because they were the ones most in denial. Kristen decided that one day of visiting should be reserved for Jesse's friends. If people showed up who weren't kids, they were nicely told to come back another time.

"I've never really been involved much in any grieving process," Jesse's friend Lee said. "Typically it happens so fast. But in this case it was weeks before the service, though in hindsight it doesn't necessarily feel that way. But it was really very important that it was so long. Every single day all of us got together—for weeks. I think that was very healthy for all of us. We just took our time about it. We didn't just try to get it over with. We just let it last as long as it lasted."

In addition to making the beautifully carved maghogany box to hold Jesse's ashes, the two Dans made a smaller, twin wooden box as well. In this box, they placed mementos of Jesse. Kristen placed this poem from her friend Anne in the box:

Jesse, we will not rush grief
For Jesse, we will linger long in the bittersweet pain of
*   memory*
We will not stifle sorrow
For Jesse, we will weep a river of tears
We will not delay joy
For Jesse, we will laugh until our bellies ache
We will not let love dwindle, for Jesse
We will kindle love with the brightness of his spirit
Sweet, sweet Jesse.

STONES

The solidity and endurance of stones offer humans comfort. In her book, *Kitchen Table Wisdom*, Rachel Naomi Remen describes a ritual she devised of giving a person about to undergo a serious operation a stone that loved ones have touched and blessed with positive thoughts and well-wishes. In Wellfleet, Kristen's friend Susan Weegar initiated another ritual of rocks, a beautiful and easily adaptable tradition. Susan describes:

When my father died about ten years ago, we gathered some stones off the beach. My mother had heard of somebody else doing this. We wanted to find these stones because my father loved the beach and he loved the water. And on each stone we wrote his name or his initials. Sometimes it was Baba, because that's what his grandchildren called him. And we put his year of birth and death on each stone. We gave them to people in the family and always had one sitting on the window sill. We still have the Baba stone, although it gets put away every summer.

When Jesse died, I wanted to do something, and I thought about the stones. So I went down to the beach and I got some stones, and my son Ben and I sat together and started writing on them. And I made some muffins and put the stones in the basket along with the muffins and brought them up to Kristen. They ate the muffins and then they were surprised to find the stones. Suddenly, everybody started making "Jesse stones." All of Jesse's friends picked it up and started making them. I didn't make that many—twenty-five or so, but once it caught on, they were everywhere. Everybody's got them.

Kristen elaborates:

What Susan did set off the whole chain reaction. Even the act of saying, "You know what, let's go get some rocks" was a call for us to go out to the beach in our grief and start focusing on rocks, picking them up, bringing them back, and watching people come and go and write on them.

I've thrown them in all the ponds around here. I've thrown them in the ocean and the bay, and I take them on trips and we leave them places. They're in pockets, and they're such great little things. I'll go into people's homes and find a rock or a prayer flag tucked in a corner. And I don't even know them that well.

PRAYER FLAGS

Following Jesse's death, Ellen LeBow, an artist and family friend, made a series of Tibetan prayer flags. Her work illustrates the way expressive forms from the world's great religious traditions are sometimes pressed into service by outsiders, transformed from cultural symbol into personal ritual. "I meant them as little prayers," she said. "I just wanted to make something physical and something that people could take after he died. And it made me think about things that symbolized Jesse, little points of imagery without words that symbolized him." They were given out at Jesse's memorial service.

The heron. I made a heron partly because of a dream that Dan had about Jesse the night before he died. The dream saw Jesse as a heron leaping up. But I also made it because he looked like a heron. He was very tall and lanky and angular. The blue heron is such a part of Wellfleet, and he is, too.

The tree. Jesse was so much like a young sapling, a narrow tree losing its leaves. The tree is also on a lot of the gravestones around here in the form of the willow or the broken branch. When a young person dies, the broken branch is shown with the leaves still on it. There is one stone that said, "Our love will accompany you," which I saw on an old gravestone in Wellfleet and put on the flag. We all thought that way.

The hand. The hand pointing up is on a lot of gravestones here. Jesse had such beautiful hands.

The Egyptian symbol. Jesse had gone to Egypt, gone scuba diving in the Red Sea, and had some romantic experiences. He talked about that adventure with such glory.

The whale. There's a whale because Jesse used to work on the whale-watching boats and loved all of the marine life around Wellfleet.

The star. I just feel that Jesse is an emanation now. He was alive, and now he's dead. He's just a power point that still keeps emanating.

THE TAPE

In the devastating days after Jesse's death, his best friends Lee, Ebb, and Dan spent time contemplating what songs to play at the service.

They decided to make a recording of Jesse's favorites. Lee, Dan, and Jesse's cousins Ab and Teo brought CDs over to Lee's father, Stack Kenny, who ran off twelve copies of a cassette tape, with songs selected from Jesse's favorites.

Some individuals are sufficiently gifted to express themselves through poetry, music, or visual art. But all of us are able to creatively locate our personality and essence in the songs and poems and paintings we love and make our own. The tape of Jesse's favorite songs conveys the essence of his carefree, reggae spirit.

1. "Natural Mystic"—Bob Marley
2. "Kaya"—Bob Marley
3. "Gypsy Eyes"—Jimi Hendrix
4. "Positive Vibration"—Bob Marley
5. "I'm Cryin' "—Stevie Ray Vaughan
6. "Getting Better"—The Beatles
7. "Stir It Up"—Bob Marley
8. "Melissa"—The Allman Brothers
9. "This Ain't Living"—G Love
10. "Burning and Looking"—Bob Marley
11. "Many Rivers to Cross"—Jimmy Cliff
12. "Tell Me"—Stevie Ray Vaughan
13. "Lively Up Yourself"—Bob Marley
14. "No Woman No Cry"—Bob Marley
15. "Pressure Drop"—Jimmy Cliff
16. "Sergeant Pepper"—The Beatles
17. "Mellow Mood"—Bob Marley
18. "In Memory of Elizabeth Reed"—The Allman Brothers
19. "Reprezent"—A Tribe Called Quest
20. "I Shall Be Released"—Nina Simone
21. "Sympathy for the Devil"—The Rolling Stones
22. "Jammin' "—Bob Marley

THE MEMORIAL SERVICE

As Jesse's family and friends entered the church, the songs from the tape played on the speakers. The service began just as Jimmy Cliff began wailing *"Many Rivers to Cross."* "I bet that's the first time Bob Marley and Jimi Hendrix have been heard in that church," Dan quipped.

Because Jesse loved birds, someone brought Jesse's cockatiel named Bird to the service. As one person put it, Bird "occasionally interrupted and occasionally accompanied" the music. The service ritualized and formalized the informal storytelling that had been ongoing since Jesse died. It brought together the rocks, prayer flags, and poems in the heightened spiritual atmosphere of a church. Kristen describes the service:

We don't belong to any church, but we wanted to do something in the Congregational Church. It's a really pretty church up on the hill. People had quite some time to get ready for the service. Our friend Sheryl started going through some of the drawers at our house, and she made three poster-board-sized collages of photographs of Jess. It was just her own little thing, and she set them up on easels at the church. Our friends did so much. When people came into the church there were flowers, baskets of rocks that everyone had painted, single prayer flags for people to take, a book to write messages. And there were these poster boards of Jess, which I know people loved looking at because very few people had a sense of his whole history. They got to look at other parts of his life, which I know they really enjoyed. We all enjoyed it.

During the service, Bill, our Unitarian minister, asked if anyone wanted to share a story. He had a dozen or so candles up on the altar, so anytime someone stood up to tell a story about Jess, he lit a candle. People told some great stories—some were reminders of when Jess was an infant, but some were from his own independent world. So, there was a lot of laughter. It was a very joyous occasion in its own way.

I remember our friend Dick Morril told a story that happened at the Duck Creek Inn. When it first opened up years ago, I worked there one summer when Jesse was a baby. Dick told about a time when he was at the desk, and apparently Jesse didn't have a diaper on. And he said that Jess started peeing—peeing on all the papers on the desk. Dick—now I happen to think that Dick is embellishing on this story a little bit—said that I swung Jess around so he would be peeing on the floor. He didn't stop peeing when I swung him, and I said something like, "I can't control him, I can only direct him." He was talking about parenting. And it did speak to my philosophy on parenting, but it was very, very funny. I do remember thinking during the service, "Is that true?"

Another story was from a gentleman who worked with Jesse on the whale boats. I can remember when Jesse would come back from working on the boats. I would love to listen to his stories about what he was learning about all the different types of birds in the ocean. And I would say, "How are you learning all this stuff?"

"Some guy on the boats told me," he would say in typical adolescent fashion.

So this man, Peter Trull, stood up and said, "We all knew the real reason Jesse was out there on those whale-watch boats was to learn about birds." It was just such a sweet thing. Here was a relationship that I kind of knew about as a parent but yet didn't have any real sense of. It was like unwrapping a little gift. People were filling out my son's life for me.

It just felt like little gifts that were being shared. It was really a beautiful exercise. And at the end, Bill lit a candle for all the stories that were still untold.

THE RESTING PLACE

In selecting a burial place, the dying, along with their families and friends, often identify key personality traits of the person who died and match those with—superimpose them upon—elements of the natural world. Jesse's burial site is an intricate collage of his life, with a vast array of symbols selected by many different people who knew him. While he was still alive, Jesse set the stage for what was to come later. Kristen explains.

For years, when Jesse was sick, I had looked into the eyes of my child and said to him, "Is this really the time you want to give up?" He'd be in pain, or tired, or throwing up, and I would say, "Are you sure? Because when you know for sure," I said to him, "you have permission from me to go. But if there's a thread of you that doesn't know, you don't have my permission. Be sure. Look at everything in you."

And when *I* knew, I asked Jess if he also knew he was dying and wouldn't be leaving the hospital. He said, "Yes." And so a little bit later I said, "So, what you would like to have happen? Do you want to be cremated or have your body put in a casket?" He said he wanted to be cremated. So I immediately started thinking, "Oh, we'll hike out to the end of Great Island or take a boat to the Red Sea and scatter his ashes." Then he said, "I don't want to be too far away, I want to be someplace close where people can come and visit."

"Jesse made the right move," Lee's father, Stack, said. "He told us, 'You put me somewhere so people can visit me.' That was the right call." His gravesite sits on a hill overlooking the graves of the early settlers, under a shady tree, where a breeze always seems to rustle the leaves. The fence around the cemetery is broken in many spots, and it's just a few steps from the road to his grave. In personal rituals, family and friends visit the site separately, bringing objects. Through their individual actions they create a collective work of art that is his grave. A bench, a Japanese lantern, shells, coins, and hundreds of meaning-laden trinkets give it the look of a religious pilgrimage site. They form a montage—an arresting, off-beat art installation.

On a cold, late-summer day, we stood with Kristen and five or six friends by the site, almost three years after Jesse's death. This gathering of people was remarkable in that, since the burial, the grave had been visited by all of them, many times, bringing objects, contemplating, reading the paper, adding knick-knacks and mementos to an ever-changing memorial. But this was the first time any of them had been here together other than the burial and the celebrations of Jesse's birthday. As Stack Kenny put it, "I've never seen anybody up here, but there's always evidence that somebody's been around."

"Who built the wall?" Kristen asked on one visit, referring to the low wall of stones that recently appeared circling part of the grave. Even *she* didn't know. In this early American cemetery, there are no other graves like this. But this unusual gravesite is having an impact, and the whole cemetery is starting to perk up, particularly during holidays.

Kristen explained some of the objects surrounding the gravesite. "The bench? Well, the wood is from his Aunt Patti's home. The oak at the base comes from Liz and Paula's backyard. Paula cut it down and dug the holes and actually put the bench up. Every little piece here has a story to it."

"My son Eben, the fisherman," said Stack, "added those scallop shells. They're beauties."

Kristen identified a rock in the shape of a heart as her contribution. She went on to explain the genesis of the site's centerpiece. "It's a Japanese lantern that a friend, Laura Brown, brought. It was part of the Summer Solstice party we had up here the first six months after Jess had died. She just showed up with it, and it's become a focal piece. There used to be a weaving here that Stack did. Stack, did I ever tell you that I would come up here and find chickadees taking pieces of the weaving out for nests?

"Mostly when I come up here I'm watering. But sometimes I come up here and either write or read the paper. I've actually never come here and seen anyone else."

"I've never come here and seen anyone else either," Lee acknowledged, "unless it's for a birthday or anniversary. But you know people are here a lot because it changes."

Kristen recounted a story about Lee's cousin Jamie who was three or four when she visited the gravesite with her mom. "Her mother was explaining to her what all these things were—because they're all treasures to a little kid. So Jamie took the barrette out of her hair and put it on the site. It's still in there."

"There's an oyster-shaped rock in there, too, from my brother

Eben," Lee said. "I can just picture him saying, 'This thing looks just like an oyster. I'm going to bring it to Jesse's grave.' "

Dennis added, "There are rocks here from beaches in Ireland, from beaches in Greece, from beaches in Italy."

"Costa Rica," Kristen chimed in.

"Portugal," Lee added.

"Because Jesse liked to travel," Dennis said, "There's a lot of money here, too—Mexican money, Italian money, Greek money, Irish money."

Kristen explained that people leave what they have in their pockets. "It could be a golf ball or Luna's dog tags."

"Sometimes you find something," Stack added, "and you say, 'I know what to do with this!' "

Shaye Cavanaugh pointed out an old hemp necklace. "I wore it for two or three years," he said, "and I came up here and I didn't have anything to put down so I put that down."

"It looks like a natural object," Kristen pointed out, "like some insect that molted its skin."

"You know," Lee said, "The whole site's not going to look like this in six months."

"It's not going to look like this in two weeks," Stack added.

Then Kristen told some stories.

Last year I made a Christmas tree for the place. When Jess was little we had a tug of war over whether to put flashing lights or plain lights on the Christmas tree. Of course I wanted plain, and he wanted flashing. So, I said, "Get your own tree—this one's in my house, in *my* living room." And he did. He took his little saw and went out to where the power line runs and sawed off a little scrub pine. From that year on, we'd go out and get a little Christmas tree for him to have in his room. He could do whatever he wanted with it. It became a really sweet tradition for us.

So the first year I put a Christmas tree up here, and we decorated it with cranberries and popcorn and then people would come up and hang things on it. Last year I made a tree with a design based on an early American image, without leaves, just the branches. I put that here and the same thing happened.

At one point, there was this elderly and very traditional woman from Wellfleet who is very well-intentioned and serves on the Historical Society. She marched into Town Hall and told them she was very upset about the gravesite up in the cemetery. She said, "They aren't following any of the rules." It's true, we did get a little list of rules from the cemetery, and we read them and thought, "They can't really mean it," and whisked them right into the wastebasket. And so this elderly woman stomped into Town Hall again to see the Town Clerk, whose name is Dawn. And Dawn told her in no uncertain terms, "There's a very nice young man up there, and you leave him alone." That's the last that was heard about it.

Last year in August I came up here and in the center, right at the bottom of the lantern, there was a small baggie that clearly had paper in it along with a pretty rock to weight it. I sat looking at it and I thought, "Should I read it? Should I not?" And I decided, of course, to read it. Whoever wrote it was kind enough to wrap it in a baggie, so clearly they wanted it protected. I still have the letter, and the rock that was in the baggie is right over there.

It was written by a woman who apparently came up here in the summertime. It starts out something like, "I did not know you in life . . ."—'cause there's no headstone at this point, there's still nothing that says who's here. But this became a very meditative place for this woman. In the letter, she talked about her own children, who had been sick but were now doing better, and about what the rock symbolized. She expressed her gratitude for having this place. It felt so vibrant and so loving to her. We don't know who she is. It was just beautiful.

Lee and I were talking today about finally putting up a stone. I know it's been almost three years, but I'm taking my time to come up with just the right design. I would put Jesse's name and dates of birth and death. I think the gravestone would be some kind of rock that is organic in shape. It actually matters to me exactly what type of rock I will get. I'm thinking of putting some animals on it, some of the ones I know were special to Jess. Or, just for a laugh, I could put his dogs and some of the birds he's known. I'll get to it. It will work out. I'm not really worried about it. I know I have to move on it someday. It's hard for me to do—it makes yet another statement about Jesse's death, and I don't feel a need to rush.

ANNIVERSARIES AND BIRTHDAYS

On Jesse's birthday and on the anniversary of his death, Kristen, Dennis, and friends continue to celebrate. The events are hardly solemn. The group often has to shush their friend Marla, who supposedly tries to get them all to sing "Kumbaya." In an adaptation, or perhaps a spoof, of a formal ritual performed in several cultures—the tradition of pouring alcoholic beverages on the ground as libations for the ancestors—they wet the ground with spilled milkshake. Kristen describes some of the celebrations.

On the day that would have been Jesse's twenty-first birthday, we went to the cemetery and had beer. Some kids brought some chips. It was so much fun because we knew that's what Jesse would be doing—sitting around, drinking beer, eating chips.

The kids had their own celebration. They had all carved pumpkins. Eben had carved one that said, "I Miss You, Jesse." It was beautiful. As it got dark, all the pumpkins were lit.

It's always the start of the "real" summer when PJ's opens up in Wellfleet. It's just a little fast-food place around here. On the first Summer Solstice after Jesse's death, we ordered french fries, a frappe milk shake, and a hamburger. We had the hamburger cut into little pieces and decorated. Then we visited the cemetery with the burger and fries and poured some frappe on the ground in Jesse's honor.

Jesse had fireworks in his closet when he died, and we ended up saving them to use on the anniversary of his death. They literally burst through the treetops. Our good friend Dan Silverman from the fire department here in Wellfleet just looked in the other direction. If Jesse were here, I could just see him go, "All right!"

Dennis explained the significance of fireworks, candles, and bonfires in their remembrance of Jesse.

On the anniversary of Jesse's death, we went to Spectacle Pond. We went with all of our friends and all of Jesse's friends. And we built a bonfire, and our friends made wreaths out of ivy. We made beeswax candles and set them in the center of the wreaths and floated the candles out onto the pond. And we sang and joked and told stories as these beautiful homemade candles floated out into the water.

Jesse died on the night of the Winter Solstice. It's so symbolic that he died on the darkest night of the year because for all of us it was the darkest night of our lives. He died right at the end of the night, just at sunrise, at the end of the darkness. In terms of the passage of the sun over the course of the year, it was the beginning of the light coming back. It was just so unbelievably appropriate, as if he had picked the time to die—maybe he did. We all sat with him through that darkness and through that night, and it was like he was helping us over until the light returned.

THE MOTHER'S DAY TEA

When Jesse was thirteen or fourteen years old, Kristen's friends Susan Weegar and Candace Perry invited her to a Mother's Day tea.

We met at one of those old-fashioned inns on the Cape that has a fancy tea service. We met a week before Mother's Day, and we've continued to do so every year since then. Sometimes we meet in someone's house and we each bring tea sandwiches or dessert. But occasionally we meet in restaurants, too. One year, a local place, Aesop's, which opens for the season around Mother's Day, opened up early for us and served us tea. We always get dressed in our tea finery. Some of us even wear dresses and hats.

The idea is for us to talk about what happened to us that year as a mother. It is an annual check-in based on being a mother. We go around the table and each of us talks. Other things come up, but there's always a report on each of our children and where they are in their lives. We also talk about where all of us are at this time in our lives and about what being a mother means to each of us.

When you go to the tea, you're thinking, "Oh God, what am I

going to wear and what am I going to talk about?" I remember getting ready for the tea just a few months after Jesse died and thinking, "Oh my God, I don't have a child to talk about." I knew they weren't going to ask me to leave, but I worried about my place in the group.

The beauty of it is that I felt very included. Even though I don't have a child to report on, I get to talk about my grief process, and I hope that I offer a voice to that which is so horrible to a mother— the loss of her child. I can open up that world, because the group responds to my pain and grief, to my story. Losing my child doesn't make me any less a mother.

It's very different for *me* to listen to moms talk about their children in middle school and college. I get to hear about the birth of another grandchild, and I get to participate in the other mothers' stories—and in their lives. We all cry at one point or another. But it's made me realize that I will always be a mother.

At one point during Jesse's memorial service, a friend got up to say, "Hillary Clinton says it takes a village to raise a child. In this case, it took a child to raise a village." Family and friends of Jesse believe his death transformed friends into family, neighbors into kin. Together, they showed how a creative outpouring of love could render Jesse's demise something other than a senseless tragedy in a meaningless world. "In my creative mind," his friend Joe Tucker said, "I can put Jesse together on a good day—I see the beauty. I see the tragedy—and yet *still* see the beauty in what he left." Through stories, rituals, and memorials, a sense of purpose was restored to the hearts of these indomitable, latter-day pilgrims on Cape Cod.

THREE

Storytelling

Rabbi Edward Schecter at Temple Beth Shalom, in Hastings-on-Hudson, New York, describes his memorial services as the inauguration of memory. "Somebody's life could be ninety years," he says, "but you have to sum it up in five minutes. You have to capture a person just right. You know how you take fine crystal glass, and plink it, and it should sound like a bell? That clear. That's how you want it to be. You want to capture a person that perfectly. Sometimes I stay up all night thinking of the right story to make that pure sound."

When those close to us die, we are charged with remembering. Our stories are memory's tools. They capture the essence of a life and make it portable. They provide a way to preserve and recall mannerisms, foibles, grandeur, and courage. The dead can no longer speak for themselves; their memories, who they were, and in some sense, who they continue to be, are with those who remain. The living give them voice.

The Dying Tell Their Story, Too

Our physical demise poses existential challenges. A dying person goes through what Michel Muzan calls a spiritual labor, "an effort to . . . give birth to one's self in the world before leaving it, to attempt to reveal one's self as one really is."

When death is imminent, many people feel an urgency to tell their own life stories, even if only to themselves. They experience an impulse to think back on their lives and to integrate their discrete experiences into a relatively coherent narrative of their time on this earth.

In 1963, psychiatrist Robert Butler, a leader in the field of geriatrics, coined the term "life review." After his important work, reminiscence could no longer be considered, as one social worker put it, "the high road to senility." According to Butler, it is the creative adaptation to a phase of life, a healthy mechanism for coping with aging and dying. Although Butler first conceptualized life review as an interior process of evaluating one's life, we and others also use the term to refer to the process of telling stories about one's life and other end-of-life art projects.

In writing about life review and reminiscence, anthropologist Barbara Myerhoff offered the term *re-membering*, to call attention "to the reaggregation of members, the figures who belong to one's life story, one's own prior selves, as well as significant others who are part of the story."

Not everyone who knows they are dying goes through a process of life review. Some people, especially those who die young, are simply frustrated and furious about what they will never be able to accomplish. Yet some terminally ill young people engage in the same reflective process as the elderly. At the age of thirty-two, Susan Landsman found herself shoved cruelly forward through life toward death. Her husband, Ron, reminisced:

In the week after we got the diagnosis, three or four nights that week we stayed up talking until two, two-thirty, three in the morning. It was like a couple of college kids talking about the Big Truths. We just spent hours talking about the life that we had lived together, recalling things done, things not done, mistakes made, times enjoyed—that's a species of storytelling.

And one time we were thinking about the things we did together, and I remember we had gone through a whole series of stories from different times in our lives. I remember I stopped and I said, 'You know, we really had a lot of fun.' And I certainly knew that, but it was really useful to have revisited those times together.

Whenever someone is dying, I think they will make a kind of review of their life, and they'll think about the things they didn't do and feel sorry for those, sometimes more than sorry. Then they'll think about the things they did do, and they'll feel their satisfactions. It's not a question of whether they met all of their goals or not. Anyone who's tried to achieve anything is also going to have many things they tried to do but didn't. It's kind of an accounting that I think almost everyone does, anyone who's at least a little introspective and who's not denying the seriousness of their problem.

Poet and therapist Marc Kaminsky observes how, through the process of life review, we can discover a redemptive "metaphor of self" that is both an emblem of the meaning of our lives and a plausible legacy.

The VA Troopers

Susan Perlstein, the charismatic director of the organization Elders Share the Arts, along with the cadre of devoted theater and visual artists she has assembled, works with groups of seniors to collect oral histories and create living history plays.

In 1985, Susan was the director of a living history theater group based in a veterans hospital in Queens, New York. She recalls that each hospital room housed four men with only curtains to separate them. A cacophony of coughs and moans echoed through the rooms as the nurses scurried up and down the halls.

The theater troupe nicknamed itself "The VA Troopers." She worked with them on a play which was taken "on the road" to other VA hospitals. Since all of its members were in long-term care, she thought of The Troopers as "liberating" patients from the hospital. Everybody wanted to be in the group. It was the only way they could leave the premises. Ambulances would take The Troopers to their performances, many of them attached to IVs or in wheelchairs or even on beds. "I had such a good time liberating them," Susan told us. "It gave them a wonderful sense of independence in their dying days."

Susan tells of her experience with one Trooper who used song in his final hours to tell his life story and chronicle his death.

COMING HOME

—Told by Susan Perlstein

Sol King was one of The VA Troopers. He was wiry with twinkling eyes and a lot of spirit. When I met Sol, he had lung cancer that had spread and had metastacized to his spine. By the time he got into The VA Troopers he was in a lot of pain and was having a hard time. But he would always say that when he was in this theater group nothing bothered him—and nothing did!

At the workshops, The Troopers brainstormed and decided to do a play about what it was like for them when they came home from World War Two; many of them, black and white, came home to confront racism and joblessness. Sol played an important role in the play because he had landed in Normandy and was an ambulance driver for the wounded. He himself was wounded in Europe, and they sent him home on a stretcher. He remembered coming home just when Fiorello LaGuardia had been elected mayor of New York. He described LaGuardia vividly, and he even played the part of Fiorello in our play.

And he remembered the song from the musical *Fiorello*, "Coming Home," which became the theme song for our play. His memories of returning home became one of the scenes. When Sol went overseas, he left behind a son who was a year old, and when he came back the child was three and a half. He never got to see his son learn to walk or talk. The Troopers actually reenacted his coming home and meeting his family again. It was a great scene—his little kid spilling things and hitting him—the son hardly remembered his father.

Since Sol was not in great shape, his wife came with him to

rehearsals and watched us develop the scenes. When we were rehearsing the play, Sol's wife came down one day and said, "Sol won't be able to rehearse today, and he wants you to go upstairs to his room—*but* he taught me all of his lines, and he wants me to play his role in the play."

It was amazing—he had rehearsed her so well that she could move right into his part. After rehearsal I went up to see Sol—he was dying—and he said to me, "You know, Susan, they're still taking my temperature, the nurses are drawing my blood, the doctors are still poking and probing. I'm dying and I know it—why don't they leave me alone?"

So I said, "Okay, Sol, I'm here with you. What do you want? I'll do whatever you want to do. I'll just stay with you."

He said, "I just need it quiet for awhile."

Then I said, "What should we do?"

And he said, "I'd really like to sing the song from our show, because I have a lot more songs to sing, a lot more stories to tell, a lot more verses to add."

So we started to sing.

"Coming home, coming home"

And then he would fill in the verses,

"The nurses are still taking my temperature
And my wife is still crying hysterically
Coming home, coming home
The nurses are still injecting me
I don't know why"

Sometimes we would pause and then start again. He added verses about his children. He wanted to talk about his wild days. The verses were all made up; they told stories in song with a chorus. He was in terrible pain. He would say, "Don't touch me because every part of my body hurts," and that was part of his song—"every part of this body hurts." We were laughing, we were crying—it was one of those moments where time stands still and every moment is forever.

We sat there for more than an hour just singing together. And then he said, "Well, I'm really tired. I think I'm ready." And I just sat with him as his breath got shorter—and then nurses came in and dragged me out of there—and he died.

I feel like Sol gave me the greatest gift on Earth. He taught me that it's through art—through singing, through poetry, through stories—that we can transcend these very, very difficult passings. He chose how he wanted to spend his last hours—he wanted in some way to transcend with music and stories and song. He taught me that creativity in people never dies—until our dying breath we are capable of transcending our own conditions.

I had a really hard time with Sol's dying because my father also died of cancer. When my father died he wouldn't talk to me, but Sol would talk to me as long as he could get out a breath. My father wouldn't do that with me. I was in college, and I really needed to talk to him, I really did. I needed to tell him things, and he would just push me away. He himself could not deal with the pain of having to say good-bye to us. Sol let me say good-bye to him. I will be eternally grateful to this man, eternally. He has no idea what a gift he gave me—that you don't have to die like my father, frightened, holding everything in, afraid to talk. He just showed me another way.

The Role of Hospice

When Sol King died in the Veteran's Hospital, nurses were still taking his temperature and drawing blood and doctors were still probing him, when even *he* recognized that, since death was near, such actions served no practical purpose. What he needed at that hour, and was fortunate to have, was a compassionate friend to be with him as he died. The hospice approach to death is a stark contrast to the traditional hospital model. Hospice aims to keep the terminally ill physically comfortable and spiritually tended to. No heroic measures are taken to prolong life.

Katherine Blossom is an innovative arts director at the nation's first hospice, The Connecticut Hospice, inaugurated in 1974. She is originally from Britain, where the hospice movement began in the 1960s. Katherine attributes the increasing popularity of hospice care to "the general population's embracing of a holistic approach to medicine and of a new interest in spiritual life." She refers not necessarily to organized religion but to a late twentieth-century Western trend toward introspection and spiritual awareness.

In her arts program, staff and volunteers encourage the terminally ill to engage with music, creative art projects, storytelling, and life review. Sometimes art is a balm that offers respite not only to the psyche but also to the body. "We've been told by patients," reports Katherine, "that during the time they're working on art projects or listening to music they don't feel the pain they were having. It's either not there at all or it's there but they don't notice it."

Sometimes art helps patients express their unspoken fears. Katherine described how the drawings of a young patient with a heart condition and Down's syndrome changed over time to reflect his failing health and imminent death.

He loved more than anything to color with markers all day long. He had huge pieces of paper and you could not interrupt him when he was doing this. He'd get very irritated and tell you to go away. We watched him for about four years. He would draw and he would cover every inch of the paper. He would never leave a piece undone and he used really bold, bright colors. There were big geometric shapes and colorful bright patterns. And then gradually, his work closed in. As he got close to the end of his life he drew in brown and black. And there were things that could be construed as coffin shapes in this brown, earthy picture. The big geometric shapes at the beginning were big and bright and open. The lines went outward. And I don't believe we should analyze everything that's drawn but his art was quite striking because the geometric shapes started to get smaller. It was a feeling of closing in, of being confined. It was really frightening to watch. And yet it was his way of dealing with his situation and approaching it. It was almost as though by repeating this image he was being realistic about it and it was easier to swallow.

With a career in the music business behind her, Katherine is a passionate advocate for using the arts in hospice settings. Her work in The Connecticut Hospice Art Department addresses the role the arts can play at the end of a person's life.

"Often at the hospice, our patients reminisce about travel—places they've visited that they know they'll never see again and there's that feeling of wanderlust. They are confined, and they can't just travel anywhere they want. Sometimes we try to satisfy their wishes. We've taken people down to the beach if that was their favorite place. There was a man who had been an avid gardener, so we took him to the garden center, and he talked about his garden. But if someone wishes to be at a place and we can't physically take them there, then we have to find a way for them to imagine it in their heads, to render it or translate it, draw it or paint it or make a collage that incorporates all of their favorite places, or to relive it in a way or tell stories about it. There's a lot of storytelling that goes on."

Katherine notes that often the patients' projects become a kind of life review for them, addressing unresolved issues in their lives. She feels privileged to participate in the ending of people's lives. "There's something very powerful about the end of a person's life that makes relationships very intense. There's incredible honesty. When you know you're going to die, you haven't got anything to lose. You've got nothing to lose except your life—and you know you're going to lose that. And that, coupled with the effects of some pain-killing drugs, reduces social inhibitions. It makes my job very rewarding. It's actually kind of an honor for me when patients let a complete stranger into their intimacies in the last two or three weeks of their lives."

"HERE I AM, HERE'S WHAT I DID"
—Told by Katherine Blossom
(Patient and family names have been changed to protect privacy.)

At The Connecticut Hospice, we work with patients grieving their own imminent death. A lot of our interactions involve creativity and life review. The whole basis of our program is that creativity, itself a kind of life force, gives people a chance to not only turn inward and look at themselves, but to turn outward and look at the whole world and review and explore.

People must come to grips with the fact that they're dying, and it helps them if they can feel that there's some kind of eternal framework around them. So making things, writing things, and looking at or enjoying things that other people have made or written or performed gives the dying a kind of hope.

The act of creating is a form of control. When you create something you choose how it's going to be. And patients who are terminally ill don't have much control over any element of their lives, and their family members often don't either. Patients often can't control their bodily functions, or what they're allowed to eat, or the fact they can't move; and they can't control the progression of the illness. But they can control the things they make themselves. They gain not only a certain kind of autonomy in that, but also pride. And it's something they can rejoice over—a good thing, a positive thing in their lives that can be otherwise very limited and confined. What's really awe-striking is when someone who's never done any art before just completely explodes and runs away with it. Their soul is so full of creativity.

Family members can see their loved ones creating and also gain great hope from it and rejoice. The creative flow is life. I think families gain some strength from that. And then they have often a tangible memento—something that the patient made or did, whether it's a painting, a sculpture, a card, a craft object, a tape recording of the story of their life, or a memory album of their life. It's something left behind for the family. Families always take the artwork home. I've never seen it get left behind or thrown out. The objects themselves are instilled with meaning and history, just like every human being is.

One of our patients, Michelle Jones, was a young mother who had a teenage daughter, Sarah. They had been estranged from each other for several years and really hadn't got along. Something had happened in Sarah's childhood, and we were never told what. But Michelle held within her this incredible grief. She said, "I feel really guilty about what I did to my daughter, what's happened to her." But she didn't ever tell us what it was. Even though we gently tried to go there she didn't want to tell us. That was fine. What she did want to do was have Sarah's forgiveness or at least get in contact with her again. So she'd called several times, but Sarah hadn't returned her calls, even though she knew her mother was here and dying. It was very hard for both of them. There was obviously a lot of unresolved pain.

Here in the Art Department we had the idea of making a memory album. We said to her, "What if you were to make a gift for your daughter, an album that could somehow say what you want to say to her that you can't say to her now on the phone because she hasn't called you back? What if your sister were to bring in small photographs and things?" Michelle's sister, who was close in age and got along well with the daughter, had offered to help.

So we took about three weeks in the making of this album, and Michelle really did a whole life review. She started from her childhood. She said, in effect, "This is who I am. I'm human. I failed you, I know. But I love you, and I want you to know that I feel sorry that you've had some hard things happen to you and I didn't mean them to happen." She said this pictorially and with poems and quotations.

When she died it wasn't quite finished. So her sister came back, which was very brave and hard to do. She came back here two or three days after the funeral and continued to work on it, and she promised to give it to the daughter when she felt the time was right.

About six months later she got back in touch with us and said she had given it to Sarah. It had been incredibly powerful and moving, and the daughter had sobbed and sobbed and accepted and was still really digesting all of it. The sister also said that it had been healing for her too, to see that the bridge had been made.

Not everyone has the impulse to review their life. Usually, for the people I've worked with who are younger, the main issue is fear of what is about to happen and fear of what is about to happen to their young children. They very rarely do a life review. It's not about what they've done or experienced or seen or achieved. It's about what they haven't had the chance to do. So there's a review of a mission rather than the actual past because there hasn't been that long a past, there hasn't been enough. Even what there has been doesn't seem worth mentioning because of the bitterness of its being taken away so early.

The younger patients are the most prolific artistically; they have this desperation to do more because their time has been cut short too soon. Those are generally the patients who are most involved in the arts program. They just work furiously day after day; even long after they're physically able, they still try. And when confusion or dementia sets in, they're still trying in a confused kind of way. "I've got to bake these breads," or "I've got to finish this picture." There's a great deal of trying to get things done. There's desperation. It's very sad to watch. It's really hard to watch. Mothers with young children facing the end are the most desperate and the saddest to watch.

Art is a good starting point for patients' introspection about their lives. I only wish people came here with more time so they could engage in these processes to a deeper degree. When you do a life review, when you present it in an artistic way, whether you write it, draw it, make an album of it, or sing it, you're stating who you are and you're making your mark. It also serves the purpose of being able to let go, because you don't do that until you've come to the point where you know it's time to do that. How many people sit down to write autobiographies unless they've accomplished something really major? For most patients, the major thing they're going to do is die—so that's when they do their autobiography. And when it's done—if it gets done—and it doesn't always—it releases the person in a way. Even the starting of it, the act of thinking that way, helps patients resolve issues they're dealing with. To be honest, it is rarely finished. It's often finished by a family member. But that, too, is cathartic for them.

For our patients, the work of life review is both humble and proud at the same time. It's the humility of letting go of this life, just letting things happen as they will naturally. It's also the pride of saying, "Here I am, here's what I did."

Living with Dying

Iolene Catalano, a thirty-six-year-old musician and former prostitute with AIDS, participated in a creative writing program run by Lila Zeiger at the AIDS Day Treatment Program in Greenwich Village.

At the very start of an interview with her about her poetry, before a single question was asked she simply started talking, delivering an insightful reflection on living with dying and the process of life review.

IOLENE'S SOLILOQUY
—*Told by Iolene Catalano*

It's funny—when you are dying you think about incidents in your life in a different way. You attempt to have closure emotionally on things that ordinarily may have taken the entire duration of a person's life. Since I learned I have AIDS, I've tried to find closure on emotional issues that I probably would not have thought about until I was *very* old. But because I'm not going to be very old, or at least it looks that way, you know, I've thought about my life; and I am surprised about the things that surface as turning points or moments of special significance to me. If someone would have asked me while I was healthy what was the most significant moment or one of the most significant moments of my life, it wouldn't have been any of these things. But since living with death as my everyday little friend, the things that I see as important now are affected by my awareness of a dark side of life.

I think that my writing before I was ill—without my being conscious of it—attempted to be happy or have something positive to say. And then, after grappling with the illness and learning to accept its effect on my everyday life, it's sort of like all this little happy horseshit that people do dropped away. Not because I wanted it to, but because the reality of living in the presence of death as your everyday little friend changes you spiritually. So you don't have this need to make reality into some little sticky, unrealistic, happy fuckin' pipe dream. It drops away, and the core or the essence of what is really important in people's emotional lives comes to the surface.

For instance, I had to come face to face with my own mortality for the years of my active heroine addiction to take on a meaning. Because that behavior, even though it looks meaningless and negative and stupid to other people, you have to realize it's the best attempt the person can make to stay alive. And if the best attempt you can make to stay alive is to punish and mutilate yourself and celebrate death through a blood ritual every day, the things that are causing you to see your life that way are really important—not just to you but to anybody.

After I started coming to the AIDS Center I wrote a poem about needles.

> *Needles*
> *all of my life . . .*
> *to get immunized for school,*
> *with a hoop and a thimble*
> *for flower embroidery*
> *on the top hems of sheets,*
> *knitting pot holders,*
> *hooking rugs . . .*
> *Needles*
> > *And then the changes.*
> > *What a mysterious*
> > *metamorphosis!*
> *"Works! Works! Works!"*
> *I can still hear Flaco*

hawking the gimmicks
on his corner . . .
in the shooting galleries,
the gaunt faces waiting
to feed the hungry veins,
staring at the bloody
cups of water holding
needles . . .

I have come to view my experiences in a totally different way than I ever thought I would, and it's a mystery to me. It's a great mystery and amazing—because what it means to me is that there is a process people go through with death. Just facing your mortality triggers something, and it causes you to start thinking in a different way. It doesn't matter if the person is five years old, if they have some concept of what death is, they can take the experiences that they have had and condense them into some meaningful fabric.

Writing poems at the AIDS Center, Lila Zeiger, the creative writing teacher, was always there for me. I think that really helped a lot. I need sort of a creative catalyst a lot of times. The poems are there, but they're not broken down into poems. Really, it's me trying to find the space where the poems are written from and be in it. Cause I don't have that much serenity in my life.

My life is really chaotic and it's unrehearsed—there's no guidelines about like how to drop dead when you're young. I have learned from each one of the other people here by watching the way they are dealing with their own mortality—I learn that the things that I'm feeling are not strange or inappropriate. I don't know what normal is for this situation. And I don't think anybody else does either.

Iolene died of AIDS in 1994. Her best friend, Cat Yellen, also a recovered addict, spoke at the memorial service at St. Marks' Church. She recounted the story of their friendship and echoed sentiments that also had been expressed by Iolene, looking back with fondness on their days on the streets. She talked first about meeting Iolene, at wild parties in more innocent times, and later on the "Ho's Stroll" on Twelfth Street in Manhattan.

"We ran together for a long time," she said at the service. "And we did a lot of destruction. You know what though? In the lowest, darkest, deepest, murkiest, delevation of addiction, we loved each other, we loved each other's souls. You know I keep flashing on all the hysterical stuff we did. We never slept. Never. And she would spaz out. You know, we'd spend all day getting a hit together and since we never slept we'd fall asleep in mid-air, holding the cooker—and she'd spaz! And everything would go flying. It's the dirtiest, darkest stuff— but, you know, I can laugh about it today."

She met Iolene again when they were both in recovery. "It's really beautiful to have relationships in recovery, but it's ultra-beautiful to have been at that level of insanity with somebody. I still have her in my heart with the two of us arm in arm, strolling down Twelfth Street, singing 'Chain of Fools.'"

The Author of Myself

Endings are crucial. The essence of a thing can sometimes be defined in terms of its fulfillment or fruition. Until we die, we are walking around without an ending. Although death represents only a single moment in a life, its position of finality often permits it to sum up the whole. People are fascinated, for instance, with last words that encapsulate lives. Numerous volumes contain the final utterances of the famous. The dancer, Anna Pavlova, who was known for her death scene in *Swan Lake*, is quoted as saying, "Get my swan costume ready." The French satirist, François Rabelais reportedly said, "Close the curtain, the farce is ended."

Daredevils such as Karl Wallenda seem to envision their own deaths in the way they live their lives. "Life is on the high wire," he once claimed, "all the rest is waiting." When he accidentally plunged from the wire in 1973 he was memorialized with lines that he might have imagined for himself: "Even in his act of dying, Karl Wallenda's performance was a celebration of his life."

Similarly, a cultural icon in a different arena, LSD guru Timothy Leary, sought to make the days leading up to his death of prostate cancer in 1996 a reverie, enhanced by marijuana, cocaine, and laughing gas. He proposed that death might well be life's ultimate altered state of consciousness.

These stories, whether apocryphal or not, suggest how much we admire those who are in control of death as the final act of living. Few of us are so lucky to die doing something we love or to end our lives with flair. Most of us are not, like Karl Wallenda, anxious to go out in a blaze of violent glory or, like Timothy Leary, in a psychedelic haze. Still, we seek to die "in character." This might mean fighting until the last breath instead of quietly slipping out of a long-lasting coma, or dying at home connected to family and friends, rather than to a life-support system.

Our lives are stories we continue to work on even as we leave them. Steve's beloved Aunt Cullough, who died a few years ago, was a consummate hostess who planned every last detail of her parties. As she lay in bed, she planned the menu for the dinner that was to take place following her funeral. She even asked her friend who was to prepare the food to bring samples to her bedside for her to taste. In her actions, she, like many others, not only found a way to die in character, but to hand her survivors her story on a silver platter.

The Storytelling Wake

Stories about the dead begin to be told as soon as people gather to remember them. When Reverend Sydney Wilde Nugent, a Unitarian minister in Washington, D.C., first sits down with bereaved families, the mourners are often in a state of shock. She works with them until the anger, memories, guilt, and pain find expression and coalesce gradually into a set of ideas for her sermon. "What is your fondest memory?" she asks them.

"If I can get that out of them and they begin to loosen that tight, closed mourning—they begin to realize that life goes on. They remember their mom and dad or their son.

Particularly if you can get them laughing, then it's not so terrible. It doesn't diminish their grief, it lets them handle it—it's still grief. For example, this one family talked about a rubber snake. It would turn up in the sugar bowl or the kids would hide it and then the mother would find it. You wouldn't hear anything about it for a while, and then it would show up in someone's shoe three days later. They told this tale with great relish, and then the two brothers got into an argument about whatever happened to the snake. It really loosened them up, and it gave me a wonderful insight into this woman who had died."

The stories told after people die are different from those told about them when they were alive. Stories become charged symbols of a person's life, and telling them becomes a ritual of remembrance. A few oft-repeated episodes have to stand for a complex individual who is no longer creating new episodes and stories.

When we tell a story about someone who has died, we remember them as alive, engaging actively in human activities. But our language, writes folklorist Kelly Taylor, reminds us that the subject of the story is dead. "In English, a dead person is properly referred to in the past tense. This subtle differentiation is a rule of which all native speakers are aware. That awareness often becomes acute the first time one must speak of someone in terms of 'was' and 'had' instead of 'is' and 'has.' "

The stories told at memorials are collaborations between the tellers and their subjects, who enacted the stories. Often in their words and actions, the dying give the survivors a ready-made set of stories to remember them by. In addition, everyone of us writes our own "death story." The details of our last days and hours will be focused on and recounted many times following our death. The death story will include our last words, details about the disease or accident or uneventful last minutes, and the exact time of death. The first question asked when a loved one dies is, "How did it happen?"

Whether the person died peacefully in bed or in a gruesome car crash, we want to know the details, the moment-by-moment chronology. We want to hear and to tell about the death in slow motion. Witnesses to the death may be asked to tell the story again and again.

Undertaker and poet Thomas Lynch has described this obsession in a poem titled "A Death," written after a friend died of a brain tumor at the age of thirty-one. It begins:

> *In the end you want the clean dimensions of it mentioned;*
> *to know the thing adverbially—while asleep,*
> *after long illness, tragically in a blaze—*

"You want to know the how, the where, what happened to whom. But the actual existential thud of it—we don't want to get near that part," Lynch told us. "And that's the part that on the one hand is the most typical—because it happens to everybody and on the other hand is the most stunning—because it happens to everybody."

The poem concludes:

> *Better a tidy science for a heart that stops*
> *than the round and witless horror of someone who*
> *one dry night in perfect humor ceases measurably to be.*

The period following a death often is so emotionally intense that humor, shattering the tension, appears far funnier than it would at any other time. Steve remembers sitting with his father and brothers when his mother was in intensive care and the doctors had given up hope. They went to dinner and, in their shock that their mother was dying, found themselves exchanging jokes about death: Sadie Schwartz loses her husband, whom she couldn't stand anyway. Although she is reluctant to do anything, her friends say to her, "Sadie, really, you should put an announcement in the paper." So she calls the newspaper and gives them two words and two words only: "Abe died." The woman on the other end of the line said to her, "Mrs. Schwartz, for our single price of ten dollars you actually get five words. Don't you want to add a few? They're free." "Okay," said Sadie, "Add this: Toyota for sale." The joke might get a chuckle in ordinary times, but on this nervous, disorienting occasion, they doubled over and laughed until they almost cried.

In another example of deathbed humor, Lynn Erdman, R.N., director of Presbyterian Hospital's Cancer Center in Charlotte, North Carolina, tells of a woman who was dying a slow but relatively painless death, sliding in and out of consciousness. The woman's two daughters were sitting patiently by her bedside day and night, waiting for their mother to die. Several days later, one of them poked the other in the ribs and whispered, "How long do you think Mom will last?" Suddenly, 'Mom' opened her eyes, looked at her two daughters at the foot of the bed, and declared, "A watched pot never boils."

When Rabbi Schecter refers to memorial stories as the inauguration of memory, he refers to life-affirming stories, not the details of death or the irreverent humor that may surface out of the devastation and shock. At memorial services and afterward, stories about a person's life begin to take precedence over stories of their death, although the way a person died remains an important episode in his or her life story. Similarly, in these stories, the sick, sometimes disfigured, dying body is replaced by images of the person in better times, alive and well, at their best. The stories of how we died are replaced by the stories of how we lived, enabling the bereaved to share memories, creating meaning on the site of loss.

Folklorist Kenneth Goldstein once described the storytelling at his father's funeral. He had returned to his parents' home in Brooklyn to "sit shiva," the traditional seven-day Jewish mourning period after burial. As a folklorist, he found himself observing how the stories told among family and friends changed over the seven days. Speechless grief gave way to stories of his father as a righteous, saint-like man; later they changed to stories of his father as an ordinary man, as "everyman." By the end, stories were told of his father as a trickster, a shrewd and funny man, good and bad by turns.

Kenny compared this personal experience with the behavior he observed while conducting fieldwork at Irish wakes. "It always began the same way. As the mourners filed into the house where the man was laid out during the wake they would always tell the family, 'You're not going to have to worry about where he's going. St. Peter's going to welcome him in.' Of course, before the wake was over, he was viewed as a mere mortal once again." His friends resumed thinking of him as part of the company, fair game for their own amusement. They placed a pipe in the dead man's mouth or dealt him a hand in a game of cards, simultaneously "joking" with him and incorporating him into the merriment.

Folklorist Kelly Taylor uses the term "the storytelling wake" to describe a variety of settings in which mourners gather to tell stories about the dead, particularly in the absence of established ritual. She proposes that these sessions, often initiated by the clergy at memorial services but continuing informally among family and friends, are an exercise in reordering experience. The deceased passes from a profane realm of immediate experience to the more sacred realm of memory. "Storytelling, like the wake ritual, is a process whereby a disordered and uncomfortable reality is reshaped into a more ordered and comfortable form."

Death and Silence

At storytelling wakes, an image of the dead often emerges which is broader in scope than the one in any single individual's mind. Tales from different times and different people in one's life help reconstruct a person of memory, a recollected soul who exists not in the everyday world but in the world of remembrance. This is beautifully illustrated in Amanda Dargan's account below of a memorial service honoring her colleague Abby. Both Amanda's story and Teresa Jordan's, which follows, speak to the power of storytelling by relating what happens when stories are absent from the days and months following a death. Amanda and Teresa point to the dark vacuum experienced when their families tried to ignore, or ostensibly forget, the death of a friend or family member.

"YOU WERE GREAT"
—Told by Amanda Dargan

I've never handled death very well. My feeling was always that any time I experienced a terrible sorrow, I didn't want anyone to know about it or feel sorry for me. I wanted to handle it privately.

My attitude about how to handle death changed when my cousin Harriet, who was a close friend of my sister Sarah, lost her father while she was in college. Her father, Woody, was a wonderful character about whom many, many stories were told. He was always getting traffic tickets for driving too slow. For the "Father's Costume Ball" at the women's college Harriet and Sarah attended, he drove up in a rented 1930s sports car filled with flowers, and, wearing a derby hat, stepped out of the car and said, "Back in those days we knew how to treat a lady."

After he died, Sarah made a point of not mentioning Woody in Harriet's presence. Sarah, like me, avoided the topic of death. Then on one occasion, she forgot herself and began telling a story about Woody before she caught herself and stopped. Suddenly, Harriet broke down and started crying. She said, "You're driving me crazy! Here my father has died, and you won't give me the chance to talk about him. You never talk about him—you never even mention his name. It's as if he never existed!" Sarah felt terrible. When she told me about this, I understood how important it is to give people who have lost someone the opportunity to talk about their loss. I realized that even more important than sharing your sympathy is sharing your fondest and funniest memories of that person.

A few years later, a woman in my office named Abby was killed in a car accident. I didn't know her that well, but I was stunned when she left the office to run an errand and then, suddenly, she was gone. She was my age and had been married only a year. She was so happy. She had had several hard years, and recently her life was going so well. She had a great husband and a wonderful future, and so her death seemed particularly senseless and tragic.

Her family had a memorial service for her at an Episcopal

Church. I am an Episcopalian myself, but I had never been to a service like this. Episcopalians tend not to express a lot of emotion at funeral services. At one point in the service, the minister said, "If any of you would like to say something about Abby you can, or if you just want to think about her silently, this is the time to do it." And I thought, "Oh no, this is awful, no one is going to feel comfortable saying anything. It's going to be embarrassing. At first no one said anything, but finally one person got up and then another. You could tell that people hadn't necessarily planned to say something, but once one person got up, other people did, too.

One woman said, "I only knew Abby in my high school, but what I remember most is that we were both into horses. And I was always very afraid, and she was so brave. She would take her horse over any jump, and because she did it, I felt that I had to be brave and do it, too. Now when I'm afraid to make a move I think of Abby, who always gave me courage when I was really frightened."

And then another woman said, "I just have one thing to say to Abby's brothers." She said, "I didn't know Abby that well, but we worked in the same office for a while. I had a new baby, and my three-year-old was having a really hard time dealing with it. So Abby wrote her a letter all about the joys of being an older sister." Then she said, "I thought her brothers would appreciate knowing that she had such wonderful things to say about being an older sister."

And then her husband got up and told about how she'd cheer him up when he was in a bad mood by placing her finger in his furrowed brow. And he told a funny story about the first time they met. He said, "The first time we met was at a big house party where everyone was crashing all over the house—on the floor and the sofas and the beds. I found a room where a woman was asleep in the bed. She was lying under the covers, so I just rolled onto the bed and went to sleep. We were both fully clothed.

The next morning we both sort of woke up at the same time, and she looked over at me and said, "Boy, you were great!" Well everyone in the church just cracked up, and it was the most cleansing, wonderful laughter.

Then her mother got up and said, "I didn't think I'd be able to say anything. I've been sitting here thinking, 'I lost my Abby. I lost my Abby.' But listening to all of you made me realize that she wasn't just *my* Abby—she belonged to all of us. I want to thank you for showing me how she touched all of our lives."

I'd gone into the service feeling so sad about Abby's death, and I came out feeling grateful for her life. It was so cathartic to be able to weep for this person but also to laugh.

Death on the Range

Ranching is a dangerous occupation. Westerner and writer Teresa Jordan recalls going for a physical and listing her injuries on a questionnaire: seven brain concussions, a broken cheekbone, a broken rib, bruised kidneys. Every get-together in the small community of Iron Mountain, Wyoming, where she grew up was, she recalls, attended by folks in "major plaster." Bones broke as often as tree limbs. But Teresa writes that the openness with which the family treated physical scars contrasted with their reluctance to deal with emotional pain. Coming from a family that did not discuss death, Teresa finally told the story of her mother's death and character on the printed page.

BONES

—Written by Teresa Jordan

At Laguna [a Pueblo reservation], when someone dies, you don't "get over it" by forgetting; you "get over it" by remembering.

—Leslie Marmon Silko

I thought my people were immortal. Deep down, I had always understood that ranch accidents could be tragic. I knew that Biddy Bonham's father had been killed when his horse tripped in a gopher hole and that old Mr. Shaffer died when he fell off a haystack. But these deaths were so distant from me they hardly seemed real. Then, when tragedy struck close to home, it had nothing to do with the roughness of our work. "The danger," my mother used to say, "is never where you think it is." Which was her way of saying, "Look behind."

The night my mother died of an aneurysm at the University Hospital in Denver, my father, brother, and I returned to the Brown Palace Hotel. It was ten o'clock at night, maybe midnight, and we called room service. I ordered vichyssoise, my favorite Brown Palace dish since childhood, and when it came, I took the silver covering off the china bowl. I sprinkled the soup with lime, as I always did, and I remember gazing at the perfect little drops of juice floating on the surface like tiny shimmering planets. I couldn't get any further, and my father, too, pushed his dinner away.

"If you can make one heap of all your winnings," he said at last, quoting Kipling, who always seemed to come to him in crisis,

And risk it on one turn of pitch and toss
And lose and start again at your beginnings
And never breathe a word about your loss . . .

And then he put his face in his hands and broke down. I remember the hugeness of him hunched in his chair. I remember a single tear breaking through the dam of his fingers, winding its way down his broad, weathered cheek to catch in his quivering mustache.

In the wide-open spaces of ranch country, animal remains are common. When you work with a young colt, there comes a day when you take him up to the bones. A colt will spook at them, even when the bones are decades old. Unless you work to overcome that fear, the colt will always shy away. There will be places in the world the colt can't walk. But if you take the time and urge the colt closer and closer, not denying its fear but not running away from it either, the horse will eventually approach what scares him. He will see that bones are just bones. He will move in the world more freely.

Ranchers walk up to most bones. They look physical danger right in the eye and don't blink. But there are other bones that scare them. For my family, the pile we shied away from was grief. Everything in my background prepared me to deal with physical pain. Nothing prepared me for emotional loss.

. . . [My father] never again shared his grief with us after we left that hotel room. We went through the automatic motions of a funeral, returned to the ranch, and sorted through my mother's belongings. Within days, we had discarded almost everything that might remind us of her.

Long before the pain had started to abate, we declared it over.

"It's time," my father said, "to rejoin the human race." I returned to college. My father met and soon married a woman who looked exactly like my mother. The marriage was painful for both partners and ended in divorce. And for years I spent so much energy denying my own longing for the dead that I hardly had energy for the living.

If any of us had a broken a leg, we would have taken all the time the leg required to heal. If the bone didn't knit in six months, we would have given it twelve. And if it still wasn't sound, we would have strapped on a brace. We might have asked each other, "How's that leg?" but we didn't ask, "How's that loneliness?" We tried to put our grief behind us, but we had only shied away from it. We started walking before we had healed. For years we hardly mentioned my mother's name. And we soon found there were places we didn't dare walk.

Story as Ritual

The act of storytelling is rendered sacred when it is set within a ritual framework. When storytelling is incorporated into rituals surrounding death, it helps focus the rites not only on an individual's spiritual existence after death, but also on his or her life, in this world. Ministers in the Unitarian church sometimes set candles on the altar and light one each time a story is told. A final candle is lit for the stories that inevitably remain untold. Minister Bill Clark explained that the candle lighting helps to initiate the storytelling; having a limited number of candles provides an end point for the telling so that it doesn't last longer than the family can bear. Lighting a candle for the tales still unexpressed can help all present feel that even their own stories, left unsaid, have been acknowledged.

The Jewish custom of sitting shiva, the seven days after burial during which mourners stay at home and community members visit to offer condolences, has often, informally, included storytelling about the deceased. More recently, some congregations have made it a formal part of shiva, written into shiva manuals, and initiated by the rabbi.

Ron Landsman lost his wife when she was still young. In his grief, he wanted nothing more "than to talk about Susan." Sitting shiva gave him that opportunity. For seven days, stories were told, framed by the morning and evening prayers. From the moment the family awoke and prayed until late in the day when they prayed again and went to sleep, all of their emotions were open, "nerves exposed," as their friend Deborah Kodish described it. The combination of religious ritual and the charged atmosphere that follows a death endowed the stories with added significance.

"What's private becomes public," Deborah said of the intense sharing of stories that enveloped them. "It was psychologically so good. I still don't know how to communicate what the texture of it was, but it's an extraordinary ritual that separates you from daily life and then lets you go back in a different way."

THE WISHBONE
—Told by Ron Landsman

My wife died tragically of cancer at the age of thirty-two. She died on Saturday night, and the funeral was Monday morning. By Monday night, we were sitting shiva, the Jewish custom of mourning for seven days. On Wednesday night there was really quite a crowd. The living room was packed by a quarter to eight. And I didn't plan this, but I began to tell a story—I don't recall for sure what it was. I was sitting on the couch that we were using as a mourner's bench, and I was telling the story to two people who were sitting close in order to listen. Then a third person began listening, so I talked a bit louder. Bit by bit, more and more people fell silent, and within a few minutes, I was telling the story about Susan to a packed room of thirty or forty people, every one hanging on my every word, utterly silent. I was totally surprised. I hadn't planned this. You could have heard a pin drop in the room. And it was great because I wanted nothing more than to talk about Susan.

As the week came to a close, one further story came to me, a story that I had pretty much forgotten about until I was telling it that night. It was about the day we found out that Susan had cancer, on Valentine's Day. Out of sheer chance we happened to have had a chicken for dinner a couple of nights earlier, and I had noticed the wishbone and had saved it. We came back from the doctor that day after getting that awful diagnosis, and were getting dinner ready. We were standing around the kitchen together, as we often did, sounding off and schmoozing, when I noticed the wishbone. And I said, "Why don't we make a wish?" I know what wish I made, and I think I know what wish Susan made. And we pulled on the wishbone, and both sides broke. We didn't say a word.

I picked up the pieces, put them on the ledge, and threw them away a few days later. We never told that story again. I can't say I blocked it out, but I didn't remember the story again until shiva week. Prayers were at eight, and I told it as the last story, just as it got to be eight o'clock. It just ended right there.

Writing It Down

In Greek myth, the hero Orpheus is endowed with great musical ability. He marries the beautiful maiden Eurydice, but their joy is short-lived. Right after the wedding, as she walks with her bridesmaids in a meadow, she is stung by a viper and dies. Overwhelmed by grief, Orpheus journeys to the land of the dead to find his bride. He uses his music to still the guards at Hades' gates and to sway Hades to return his bride to him. Eurydice is returned to him on one condition. Orpheus must not look back at her as she follows him up into the light of the upper world. Just as he breaks into the daylight, however, he turns to make sure she is still behind him. He watches as she fades back into the darkness forever.

In Greek myths, heroes are capable of physically journeying to the land of the dead. In our time and place, mourners sometimes make such journeys in their imaginations. Sometimes they make their voyages in a dream or in a piece of writing. Eric Miller's sister died when she was sixteen and he was fourteen. "I had to identify her body," he told us. "She had fallen or jumped from the roof of the building in which our family lived, into an alley, near 55th Street and 7th Avenue in Manhattan. Perhaps she jumped: she had attempted to take her life several times before. She was angry at our parents and at society. One of her complaints was that people were just too cold and isolated and alienated and uncaring. I wrote a play about it. That was part of my mourning process. I wrote a play about a boy who goes to find his sister in a kind of black void, and asks her why she left the world."

Wun Kuen Ng was born in a small village in Canton province.

Her brother, who was a year older, died when she was a little girl. For years she was told that he was swimming in the river and drowned. "It was not until I was twenty or twenty-one that my Aunt Yam told me that he was playing by the well with my older sister, Ching-Ching, and fell in. All I can remember about it is that they placed his body belly side down over a water buffalo. It's a Chinese superstition to do that, and I have a mental picture of it."

When Wun was seven years old, the family immigrated to America. Years later Wun felt a need to talk about the feelings that were never expressed when her brother died. Talking about the feelings with a therapist gave her the opportunity to belatedly mourn her loss. As she described it, "It broke open my emotional womb, and it was painful coming out."

Wun decided to write a story from the perspective of the boy who died. Wun's story, "The Wishing Well," is written as a message from her dead brother to the world that did not sufficiently acknowledge his death. In one part of her story, her dead brother writes a note to the family, forgiving them and offering his blessings to each family member, including Wun, nicknamed Wantty:

Daddy, there was nothing you could have done to save me. You are a great father.

Mummy, I know it was hard to lose me but you have always been a strong mother who will live for her children's sake.

Khan, you have accomplished so much. Do you know I read the classic stories of the Three Kingdoms all by myself?

Ming, I ate as well as you do. I always thought of you on New Year's Day when there was a huge feast with stir-fried lobsters, curried chicken, black bean clams, and my favorite: fish with scallion, ginger, and soy sauce.

Ching-Ching, no one blames you. Such large responsibilities for a little person are unfair.

Who knows the ways of the universe?

And my little Wantty, whom I did not have a chance to say good-bye to, you often sat waiting for your big brother to come home. In your mind's eye, I never left you.

Wun, as the author of the story, is speaking to herself, of course, coming to terms with her brother's death, and forgiving her family. Thinking about what her brother might have to say about his death helps her interpret it for herself. He is her muse.

Dreams

The dead sometimes appear to us in our dreams. Many of us think of such dreams as a form of communication between the realms of the living and the dead and interpret them as messages. Of the myriad dreams we dream each night, often one is picked out because of its resonance and explanatory power. By interpreting the dream and telling it as a story, the dreamer gives it significance in his or her life.

Writer Susan Horowitz told the story of encountering her father in a dream.

My dream of my father happened about a month after he passed away. It was long and had many parts, but in the end I remember that my father lay down on the bed and I said to him, "Daddy, please don't be sick, please don't die."

And he said, "Some things just can't be helped."

Then I sank down on my knees and he gave me an enormous bouquet of flowers. And then he closed his eyes.

Susan believes the dream was telling her not to think she could have prevented his death. A few years earlier, she felt that she had saved his life by convincing him to have heart surgery, which he was stubbornly refusing. The operation undoubtedly prolonged his life.

In the dream he came to tell me, "You don't have to do it again. You don't have to prolong it again. Your job is over. It's time for me to go."

I think I had to hear that because I believed in a certain way that keeping him alive was on my shoulders, and that I had that kind of power and responsibility. And this was his way of saying, "Some things can't be helped. It's not your job to keep me alive. I'm going."

When he gave me the flowers, I felt he wanted to free me from any sense of guilt I had about any of our conflicts in the past or about his death—especially because I was away on vacation when he died. It was his way of telling me that he loved me and wanted me to be free and happy.

It's very curious to me. I'm crying as I tell the story, but in the dream I wasn't crying. I was happy. It was a happy dream.

Coincidence as Communication

Certain dreams are readily interpreted as communications from the dead. Perhaps more subtle, yet just as prevalent, is our interpretation of coincidence as a medium of communication. It often seems so unlikely that coincidences would occur randomly that it seems more reasonable to view them as signs from God, from the dead, or from the universe. Many of the stories we tell about coincidences bestow such meanings upon them.

Events accrue meaning when they happen at the same place, at the same time, or on the same date. Sometimes a clock is said to stop or a plate is said to fall off the wall at the time of death. When two potentially unrelated incidents happen at precisely the same time, on the same date, or in the same place, they are sometimes connected in the minds of those who observe this potentially random precision. Coincidences are woven into stories designed to demonstrate that the unusual coalescence of events makes sense within the larger scheme of things.

The narrative structure of real life is a sharp contrast to crafted fiction and folktales. As sociologist Erving Goffman writes, "Tales, like plays, demonstrate a full interdependence of human action and fate—a meaningfulness—that is . . . not necessarily characteristic of life." But as human beings, we like to think of our lives as crafted; we seek out the artful in real life. In stories about coincidences regarding the dead, there is a sense of the uncanny and yet there is also a sense that it is aesthetically pleasing. It is tidy.

Carl Jung coined the phenomenon *synchronicity* to refer to "the simultaneous occurrence of two meaningfully, but not causally, connected events." He distinguishes this from *synchronism*, which simply means the simultaneous occurrence of two events. Some scholars, like Jung, argue that the meaning is actually outside the psyche, part of a master plan for the universe; others argue that we provide the structures of meaning in our own minds.

Steve and Debra are a couple who served as guardians for Siamese twins brought from the Dominican Republic to the United States for surgical separation. As reported in *New York Magazine,* "Their own son Shawn had been killed in a drowning accident some years earlier. It was 2:06 in the afternoon when Steve and Debra's son Shawn was born; and it was at 2:06 P.M. that the twins were separated. A woman of deep spiritual feeling, Debra began to think of Shawn as an angel watching over the girls' well-being."

This type of mental association sometimes turns into a story in which two conceivably unrelated events are told as part of a single narrative. Doris Ullendorff described how she and her husband Ken Gorfinkle were inspired by a coincidence to create a comforting story about their son Ari, who died at age one and a half. After Ari died, the family said *Kaddish*, a Jewish prayer that is recited by mourners every day for eleven months after the burial of their dead.

"The amazing thing was that our son Gabriel was born eleven months after Ari had died. And his due date was the last day for saying the *Kaddish* prayer for Ari, which I found totally bizarre—just the odds of that coming out are so unlikely. And so on the last day of saying *Kaddish*, we went to *shul* (synagogue) and brought bagels for a breakfast to honor his memory. Gabriel was born the very next day. He was born at one o'clock in the morning—just into the next day. And on top of that, it was Friday the thirteenth. There was something just really unusual at play.

"At Gabriel's bris (ritual circumcision) we said that their two souls had crossed. Some say that the end of saying Kaddish is when the soul finds its resting place. So we said their two souls had crossed—one finding its resting place and the other one just arriving. We joked that one told the other, 'Don't worry—I've broken them in.'"

Judithness

A few months before she died at the age of thirty-six, Judith Obodov Hardin made a pact with her husband, Moh. This pact led him to interpret an unusual incident after her death as no mere coincidence. For three years she had fought breast cancer with all the chemotherapy and radiation that Western medicine could muster. She also tried natural healing, even a Native American shaman in Colorado. Each variety of medicine left not only physical but also psychological scars. Western medicine encourages self-examination and regular check-ups for early detection, so Judith had to cope with the guilt of not having visited a doctor sooner, the sense that it was all her fault. Alternative medicine, on the other hand, often demands complete faith in nontraditional healing techniques; when they failed, the responsibility was once again on Judith. As a young Native American friend mentioned to her, the shamanistic healing rituals might have failed because she didn't believe in them strongly enough.

She answered bluntly, "Alex, I'm at a place in my life where I am facing my death. I didn't choose to be here. I am not here because I gave up. This is not bad. I do not feel bad about myself; it just is what is. When I die, it is not a defeat. Believe me. I have tried everything, and right now I am facing my death.

"Someday, you'll be here. I don't care how many spirits you have out there, how many ceremonies you do, and how much you pray—you are going to die. Sam is going to die; all of your medicine men have died or are going to die. The Indian way has helped me very much, but a real warrior sees that death is not giving up. A real warrior knows that someday we are all going to die."

Judith's final months, chronicled beautifully by Marilyn Webb in the book, *The Good Death*, were laden with intimacy. Judith read novels aloud with her husband and children. At night, she and Moh would read Buddhist philosophy and talk about dying in tones that were alternately serious and playful. As Webb writes, "They made a pact. Judith joked that if she could—after she left her body—she'd make the pictures hang crooked on the walls of her bedroom. Connie, the most meticulous of housekeepers, was sure to notice! She also agreed to let them know as much as she could what it was like to die as she was in the process of actually dying."

As her family surrounded her bedside in her final hours, Moh noticed that she pointed to her mouth. He rushed to offer her a sip of tea, then a sip of water. Then he realized that she was telling him that she could no longer talk. A few minutes later she pointed to her eyes. This time Moh asked if she needed her glasses. Then he realized that she was telling him that she could no longer see. She was living up to her part of the bargain. When she died, Moh said his strongest reaction was that there was no more "Judithness."

Then, on the day before the funeral, the housekeeper asked Moh if he noticed the pictures. "The pictures on the wall over Judith's bed. They are crooked." Some of them hung at more than a 45-degree angle.

"The time around Judith's death felt very magical," Moh later recalled. "It didn't take away the loss or the grieving. When she died I felt like a wide open slit had been cut through my heart. But these things, these funny coincidences, were there."

Michael and Margaret

Michael Walsh, a horse-trainer, farmer, and local historian in County Waterford, Ireland, forged a satisfying story out of coincidences and unusual events. The first part of Michael's story tells of a conversation he had with his wife, Margaret, prompted by seeing a mock séance on a television commercial, in which she promised to send him a sign from beyond the grave. The second part of the story is his discovery of her sign. It is a beautifully crafted narrative of love, loss, and faith. Michael told the story as he sat by his crackling hearth, speaking of his adored wife, now dead and gone.

"I'LL SEND YOU A SIGN"
—*Told by Michael Walsh*

I don't know if she knew that she was going to be ill or not . . . But there was an ad on the television for Lemon's Pure Sweets.

There was a seance. They all put their hands on the table and the witch woman said, "Now Jack, if you're well up there . . . send down word to us now about how you're getting on there. Are ye *there*, Jack?"

And a *whole* lot o' Lemon's Pure Sweets fell down on top of their hands.

"*My goodness*, Jack must be having a great time above in heaven!" they say. "*All* the Lemon's Pure Sweets he has up there. He could throw down a whole bag."

And the wife was having an orange there and I was having another here. And she was peeling the orange with a knife.

And she said, "Now, if you died before me and got up to heaven, would you send back word to me like that about how you're getting on above?"

"Well," I said, "If I died before you I wouldn't be let back anyway. But putting it the other way, if you went before me," I said, "Would *you* come back?"

"Well now, 'tis like this," she said, "I would if I could. And you can take it from me now that if I ever die before you, that if I can, I'll give you some kind of a word, or a *sign* . . . if you ever see a sign, if I die before you, it'll be from me."

Now no one ever knew about that. Only the two of us. . . .

And . . . she was three weeks gone. She was four years unwell. She was three weeks gone and my daughter Florence came in. She was sweeping the house and tidying up and washing things.

She said to me, "Dad," she said, "Mommy's tree is going to fall down now out there if the vine comes heavier. And you should go out now and tie it back because she'd be asking you to do that now, if she was here."

'Twas a kind of an annual thing to tie back this tree. 'Twas a rather nice tree with lots of flowers hanging down out of it. I tied it up every year for her. And I went out and I tied it back. Then I saw the hedge was hanging out. This hedge was a thing that produced flowers like dandelions.

So I said, "Now that I'm at it at all, I might as well tie back the hedge, too. 'Twill fall." See?

So I went down to push it back in. And there on the hedge was a magnificent mat of beautiful yellow roses, growing on the hedge . . .

And I looked at it and I said . . . , "Roses, my God."

I couldn't believe it.

I said, "Merciful Lord God." "I'll send you a sign, if God will allow me I'll send you a sign." That's what she said.

And I backed away from it. I got a fright. I was thinking about the wife and she telling me about the *sign* she was going to send.

And I went back again and I said, "No. People will think I'm gone in the head, ye know, and that I'm not well since she died and so on. If I went in and told Florence that now, and Florence came out and no roses to be there, they'd put me into a mental home. Wouldn't they—like, you know?"

I was saying this to meself.

I said, "I'll say nothing now until tomorrow . . . If they're there tomorrow morning, I'll tell Florence. I don't care what'll happen after that."

Well I went out at half seven the following morning. I went down and I looked. And there was about another half foot added on to the end of it. 'Twas about nearly two feet long.

So I counted it, as much as I could. And there was a rose, or a bud of a rose, for every year of her life . . .

And I left them there and I was thinking what will I do about it.

I went to look at it every morning. And I was looking one morning and they were all starting to wither. They were getting burnt with the frost. 'Twas only the end of April now, 'twas only late April. And, seldom you see roses of *any* kind in April. But this was the end of April, 'twas three weeks after she had died.

And . . . I told Florence. Florence came over and she saw them.

She said, "That's extraordinary," she said. "Can I tell Rita?"

I said, "Do tell Rita."

Rita came down—another sister—and the two of them were looking at it. I was peeping down at them, you see, and observing their attitude, you know.

And I went down and I said, "What do you think of that? What is it?"

She said, "Dad, there's only one thing I could think about that. Mommy must be in heaven and she's trying to tell us."

They never knew about the talk between their Mommy and me.

This story demonstrates a relationship between man and wife and between Man and God. Michael feels certain that God exists and that his wife is in heaven because God allowed her to send him a sign. The association of the unusual bloom with his wife was strengthened by the fact that the roses appeared near her tree, a place that had been associated with her while she was alive. The association was bolstered even further when the number of blooms was felicitously found to coincide with the number of years his wife had lived.

Trump Cards and Rainbows

We often feel that the dead communicate with us through coincidence even if they don't tell us in advance that they will send us a sign. Max Gimblett's aunt, an inveterate card player, lived in New Zealand. Max, an artist, lived on the Bowery on New York's Lower East Side. A few days after her death, Max found a brand-new playing card, a three of spades, outside his front door on the Bowery. This was her ultimate trump card in the games of whist they played together. "It was a sure sign that she'd passed to the other side," he said.

Lois Wilcken spent a day after her father's funeral on a "pilgrimage" to places that she shared with him. A coincidence on that day provided her with the raw material for a story. "One of those places in Staten Island," she told us, was Martling's Pond, and I went from there to the Staten Island Zoo where he had taken us, and I visited the first house I lived in when I was born. I just walked up and down that block. It had been a rainy day and I could tell it was going to get dark soon. But as I walked past the pond on the way home, the sun was breaking through the clouds, and I looked up and saw this perfect rainbow, a perfect arc with perfect colors. When I saw it, I remembered that on the day of my mother's wake just a few months earlier, leaving the house for the funeral parlor I also saw a rainbow. But that time there was just one leg of a rainbow that tapered off. I don't see rainbows very often, and I don't know if I've ever seen a full rainbow before this. When I saw the full rainbow, the first thing I thought of was Mom and Dad, reunited, holding up the two ends. I took it as a sign that they were up there together somewhere."

Homo Narrans

Barbara Myerhoff suggested that humankind might be considered, above all, *Homo Narrans*—narrators, storytellers. We identify meaning in the world as we experience it, and we make those meanings manifest in our stories. As human beings we are committed to artfulness in our lives, because that artfulness provides us with a rubric of meaning. We might attribute phenomena like the blooming roses or the crooked pictures to the supernatural, to an overarching cosmic order, or merely think of them as coincidences that make great stories. When we open ourselves to coincidences, we, in a sense, allow the universe to tell its stories with a vocabulary of interconnected events that we must interpret in order to grasp its meanings. Just as Rumpelstiltskin of folktale fame spun straw into gold, we spin meaning out of the straw of real life.

The gossamer bridge of story delicately spans the chasm between life and death. Families and friends work on bridging the gap from both sides. The dying review their own lives, pass on their own stories, and shape their words and actions to fashion a suitable ending for their life story. On the other side, loved ones select and embellish the stories to remember their dead; they stumble upon and interpret coincidences and dream dreams in which the dead communicate with them across the divide. Made of dreams, happenstance, and memory, stories build bridges only in our minds. Still, these ethereal constructions bear the weight of sorrow. Stories are a way—one of the only ways we mortals have—of surviving our deaths and of carrying our loved ones with us wherever we go.

FOUR

Ritual and Ceremony

Rituals are serious business. They effect change in the world. They demonstrate who we are and who we must become. A ritual can transform a man and a woman into husband and wife. Rituals provide formalized, socially acceptable responses at the most critical junctures of our existence. They dictate how to behave at the best and worst moments of our lives.

Rituals are dramatic. Like theater, they affect our emotions and are laden with symbolic action. Although rituals are akin to theater, as sociologist Erving Goffman points out—in plays performers appear as characters other than themselves; in ceremonials, we play ourselves in one of our central roles. The dramatic quality of a ritual such as a wedding, for instance, provides ways for people to experience themselves in the roles of bride and groom. Such performances of our identity help us understand our place in the world with greater clarity. "In ceremony and in fiction, we find what is missing in experience—a beginning, middle, and end," write literary scholars Maura Spiegel and Richard Tristman.

Rituals help us pass from one state of being to another. Rituals surrounding birth incorporate the new life into society. Initiation rites incorporate children into adult society. Funerary rites first separate the deceased from the land of the living and then help incorporate them into the world of the dead. Mourning rituals separate the bereaved from the rest of society. After the culturally prescribed period of mourning is over, rituals help mourners become reintegrated into society. Rituals, like stories and commemorative art, can also be used to integrate the dead into the world of the living. Many people who have lost loved ones have created their own rituals toward this end.

When people create new rituals, writes David Kertzer, they usually create them out of pre-existing symbols. The power of ritual, says Kertzer, stems from its basis in a particular social group and in shared psychological associations and memories.

After the death of their son Ari at the age of one and a half, Doris Ullendorff and Ken Gorfinkle incorporated his memory into traditional Jewish rituals in ways that keep him an integral part of their family life. Doris described the evolution of these family customs. The first was connected to the ritual of lighting candles on Friday night to usher in the Jewish Sabbath.

When Ari was born my brother gave me a set of candlesticks with the intention that the child would light them every *Shabbat*, and then, when he grew up and left home, he could take his set with him. So of course when Ari died we didn't know what to do with his candlesticks, but we felt that it was important to keep lighting them.

When our other kids were born, they also each got a set of candlesticks. And so every Friday when we light our candles, Ari's set gets lit too. So it's kind of like a weekly thing that Ari comes to visit.

Lighting Ari's candles at first, without any other children, was very weird. But it felt really important to do it, because we felt somehow that if we didn't do what we had done before, when he was alive—we had this fear that somehow the essence of him would disappear, would get lost. So the candlesticks are really important. And I think about how some day, when the kids grow up and leave and take their candlesticks, his will still be there—which is a strange thought—that his will always stay.

Doris and Ken also incorporated Ari's spirit into their *seder*—the ritual meal held on Passover. They were prompted by the traditional belief that the prophet Elijah visits Jewish homes during the *seder* and drinks from a *kiddush* cup, a ceremonial wine cup, set out for him on the table.

Another thing we've done is that we always put Ari's *kiddush* cup next to Elijah's cup at Passover time. Because if Elijah's going to come in and visit, then we figure *his* spirit should come visit, too. [Doris laughs.]

I think that had to do with the timing of Ari's death. Because within six or seven weeks of his death it was Passover. Well, there was no way we could possibly get through a *seder* without having him present. Putting his cup on the table was a way to include him at the table. It just felt so empty.

THE *BEAU GESTE*

Both personal and community rituals have their place in our struggles with death. Many scholars believe that the power of ritual lies in community—in our shared participation and emotional involvement in a group. Folklorist Erika Brady, however, has studied personally composed rituals of grief that often are created specifically when community support is absent. Sometimes, the community at large does not sanction the relationship of the mourner to the deceased; in these instances, grief and love must be expressed covertly.

Erika Brady writes of a man who lost his gay lover to AIDS. The dead man's family, as next of kin, was in charge of the funeral arrangements. His lover, feeling the need to be involved, managed to conceal a small lucky charm, that he had given the dead man as a gift, in the hollowed-out heel of one of the shoes in which he was buried. Such acts are almost subversive in their discreet challenge to family members who claim exclusive rights to the deceased.

Sometimes, a personal rite is simply "an intimate act between the dead and living person not to be shared with others." Erika Brady writes of a widow who, after agreeing to remarry, tearfully dropped her first wedding ring into the ocean as a symbolic gesture, at that bittersweet moment in her life.

In another instance, recounted to Brady, "The sister of a man who died kept his tobacco pipes long after she had disposed of his other belongings. She couldn't figure out what to do with them. She finally made a little boat for them out of cardboard covered with aluminum foil and put them out to sea on his birthday."

Many personal rituals of grief involve the "reverent and symbolically charged disposal" of items associated with the dead. Immediately after a death, such items are generally buried with the dead or left at their graveside. After some time has passed, items are burned, dropped into a body of water, or set out to sea. Such acts seem to consign items of symbolic significance to the cosmos, signaling a reconciliation to the loss and a readiness to resume daily living.

Erika Brady calls such personal rituals of grief examples of the *beau geste*, selecting the name from a novel by Percival Christopher Wren. The French term *beau geste* means "grand gesture." The *Beau Geste* of the title represents both the hero's nickname and a deed done by Beau for honor's sake.

As children, Beau and his brothers loved to stage Viking funerals, placing tin soldiers on toy boats and setting them aflame on the water. When Beau dies heroically as a soldier in the French Foreign Legion, one of his brothers improvises a symbolic Viking funeral.

The *beau geste* is private rather than communal; it can be highly unconventional, as it often is found in instances where conventional expressions of mourning fail to satisfy. And perhaps above all, it has personal symbolic significance. Erika Brady illuminates its power: "Expressing the importance of one person, one relationship, one life, each *beau geste* is a little essay on a particular loss, quietly defying the powers in life and death that level distinction."

The creative aspect of ritual is highlighted by Richard Shechner in his phrase, "Ritual is the encounter between imagination and memory translated into doable acts of the body." The pages ahead tell of deaths at different ages throughout the lifecycle, from a miscarried baby to a ninety-five-year-old man. For each loss, family and friends collaborate, sometimes with the person who dies, to translate imagination and memory into action through rituals that reorder their worlds in ways that mitigate the finality of death.

Stillborn

The reality of loss that expectant parents experience when a woman suffers a miscarriage often is not acknowledged by society. When a woman gives birth prematurely to a baby who is not viable outside the womb, to a stillborn baby, or to a baby who dies shortly after birth, society is slightly more sympathetic. Yet, traditionally, no formal rites have been developed to acknowledge these deaths. Perhaps this is because, at one time, infant mortality rates were so high. Perhaps it is because in some religious belief systems a baby is not considered a full human being until it attains a certain age. In Jewish practice, for instance, a baby who dies before the age of thirty days is not considered 'a person' to be mourned in the traditional way. Some individuals who have felt the need to mark their stillborn or newborn babies' deaths have created their own funerary rites.

"WE HAD TO DO SOMETHING FOR THIS CHILD"
—*Told by Susan Knightly*

Leonard and I had been trying to have a baby for years. Josh was just three weeks from his due date when we lost him. You know, the minute you feel a child kicking inside, you give it a personality. When the baby heard certain music he responded, and when my husband Leonard came into the room, he would respond with a kick.

The day of my miscarriage, I was home by myself. Suddenly, I sneezed and I felt a sharp pain and this bubble moving inside me. I got extremely flustered and called 911. I don't remember what I said on the phone, but this wonderful telephone operator, who figured out the situation, tried to calm me down. She started singing *"Amazing Grace"* to me, and she was singing on the phone and praying, trying to sustain me till the ambulance arrived.

Josh was still alive when we reached the hospital. When he was born, I was awake enough to see that he was moving, then I blacked out. Some time later, the nurse came in. She had washed him and wrapped him, and when I opened my eyes, I saw he looked just like my husband. He had his eyes, and his feet, and his nose. It was so touching. Then the doctor came in looking very uncomfortable and I realized that the baby hadn't made it.

"What do we do now?" I asked.

"We send him to Staten Island," the doctor said. "When babies are born who haven't breathed on their own, that's where we usually send them."

My husband, Leonard, later explained that it was a dump.

As I lay there and looked at my husband, both of us were weeping. What made it even sadder is that I could hear the sounds of healthy, crying babies on the ward. Suddenly, we both knew that we had to do something for this child. I have always found that ritual helps any passage in my life; ritual has always sustained me, and this was a time when I desperately needed it.

Someone put us in touch with the Parkside Memorial Home, and they told us that they would arrange for the burial of the baby without charge. They were so nice. The nurse brought the baby the next day, and we washed the body. My husband wrapped Josh in his own bar mitzvah *tallis* (prayer shawl). He felt that he wanted to do that. The doctor was horrified.

We had a full-fledged funeral for our child. We read poems, and friends played their instruments, and we placed the poems in the casket with him. We even took a small sculpture from our backyard and put it over his grave in Cypress Hills cemetery. We created a real feeling of life and death, of completion.

Even though the Jewish religion doesn't call for it, we sat shiva (the seven-day Jewish mourning period). I got to cry with witnesses, and I felt safer than I'd ever felt in my life. I have these wonderful women friends who attended, and I sensed they would hold me if I fell. Each of them shared stories with me about birth and about loss. All these women had suffered substantial losses. The whole invented ceremony had enormous meaning for me. I truly believe that ritual and stories are a way people can heal themselves in situations where loss is overwhelming.

When Susan Knightly lost her baby, her mother shared with her a loss of her own. "My mother was able to talk about it for the first time," Susan said, "to let me into a part of her life that she never shared with me." Her mother's baby lived for only four days. When it died, Susan's father made all the arrangements, went out to the cemetery by himself, and took care of the burial. "That was the way it was done," Susan said.

Stillborn babies often have been buried without any formal ritual. Hospitals used to view such babies and miscarried fetuses as tissue to be disposed of. Some still do. Hospital personnel would whisk those babies away without ever even showing them to their parents. The possibility of parental attachment to their unborn children, whose arrival had been so eagerly anticipated, was not acknowledged. Today, hospital social workers often try to help parents of stillborn babies with their loss.

At New York's Beth Israel Medical Center, secular rites have been developed based on the notion that remembrance is an important part of grief. One of the ways people progress through the mourning and grieving process is by reliving memories of good times with the person who has died. Memories offer a degree of comfort. When a baby is stillborn or a fetus miscarried, no such memories exist.

The Beth Israel staff endeavors to create remembrances of the babies for the families to have as keepsakes. The baby is wrapped in a knitted blanket and clothed in booties and a hat. The family is asked if they would like to hold the baby. Photos are taken. Footprints are made. The blanket, booties, and hat are offered to the family, as things that have touched their baby, to serve as mementos. The hospital also offers the photographs and footprints. Sometimes, parents will reject the photo at first but will call much later to see if they might have it after all. The hospital keeps these on file for several years so they can accommodate such requests.

Portraits of the dead might seem morbid to some sensibilities. In Victorian times, however, paintings or photographs were often made of children when they died. Sometimes, these were the family's only image of their child.

The Feeling of Empty Hands

Ari Gorfinkle died suddenly at the age of one and and half. "The most baffling thing about losing someone you love," said his father, Ken, "is that they're physically not there anymore. And you want to touch something." The bodily absence of a loved one is more acutely felt, perhaps, in the deaths of little children. "Ari was a baby when he died. I didn't have conversations with him. My interaction with him, my experience of him, was that I had held him, carried him, changed him. The feeling of empty hands is what I was left with. My wife Doris and I wanted to hold more babies. We needed to. And we had three more babies in the next four years."

In accordance with Jewish tradition, Ken went to synagogue every day for eleven months after Ari died to say the memorial prayer for his son. There he discovered that the physical action of a traditional ritual, the act of wrapping the leather straps of his phylacteries (*tefillin*) around his arm seven times in preparation for prayer, took on a new meaning. "Although I had laid *tefillin* before, it was a foreign experience. As a mourner it became an *unforeign* experience. When grieving the death of a child, you are totally numb—emotionally and physically. But when you wrap *tefillin* around your arm, it makes you feel alive in a very particular way. And you can wrap it as tight as you want, depending on how you're feeling. I wrapped *tefillin* around the same left arm that I carried Ari with. And over the course of eleven months the sensation of being alive that I got from the *tefillin* tempered my numbness and connected the feeling of the *tefillin* on my arm to the process of healing."

Designing Death

Often, the way a person chooses to leave this world is expressive and emblematic of who they were in the world. It epitomizes their essence. In the book *Intimate Death,* describing her work in hospice, Marie de Hennezel recounts the death of a bedridden dancer named Jean.

"Just before he died, Jean sent for his friend. He asked him to hold his hands and dance with him. He wanted to remain a dancer to the very end. Jean lifted himself a little and with his friend's help began with all his heart to make his arms dance, while his friend wept uncontrollably. 'Dance, dance,' he kept saying as their linked arms swayed from left to right. Then Jean smiled a magnificent, transcendent smile and collapsed back onto the pillow. He had died in his dance."

"Death and our participation in it can be experienced as fate or as act, as the lack of us or as the fulfillment of us" writes Donald Heinz. He proposes that, "If life review invites the narrative construction of the self, ritual invites the performative construction of the self." Our death must be our own.

People who are terminally ill or very old can exert some control over when they die. An unusually high number of elderly people died right after New Year's Day 2000. Those people wanted their lives and life stories to extend into the new millennium, according to one theory. When we die on meaningful dates or in meaningful places, death becomes more dramatic than it already is.

Liza's Story

Death is a rite of passage. It entails movement. It requires us to leave this world. Some people orchestrate their leave-takings in dramatic ways. Later in this section, we meet Jacob Koved, who willed to live through his ninety-fifth birthday. His "backstage" dying during his party became a theatrical production. Liza Lister willed to live through her sixth birthday. Liza staged her death scene in advance and even rehearsed it in her own way.

Liza Carolina Lister was diagnosed with leukemia on the eve of her fourth birthday and died twelve days after her sixth birthday. She had a precise picture in her head of how she wanted to die, and with the help of her family, she successfully directed her own death scene. Her parents, Elena and Philip, and her siblings, Molly and Solomon, have created memorials and family rituals to keep her life present in their lives.

Liza's mother, Elena, told Liza's story at the Lister home in New York City, in the room where Liza spent her last waking hours with her family. A cow-shaped candle rests on the countertop. Liza loved cows, and every year on her birthday her family lights a cow candle at supper in her honor. Liza's collection of stuffed cows is upstairs in her father's closet where she left it. She slept in her parents' bed at the end of her life and arranged her cows in the closet near the bed to be near them at night. "And we've never moved them. They're still there," says Elena. "So my husband's always rummaging for his shoes amidst cows," she laughs. At the end of her life Liza was day-night reversed and would go to sleep at three in the morning. "One night she came up to bed and nudged me and handed me something. And I was sort of in this groggy half-sleep state. It was a cow. 'I want you to have this. This is gonna be for you.' It's one that I keep in my office with me."

Liza left behind another parting gift as well. She had expressed a wish to go to a "paint-your-own-pottery" studio before she died, and Elena organized a family "pilgrimage." "We all made something that day, which we still have. But I refuse to use them," says Elena. Liza's piece of pottery is painted with a big heart surrounded by purple elephants. "Elephants were always representations of me because I'm an elephant collector the way she was a cow collector," explains Elena. "It's something she made knowing that we would have it after she left."

A book titled *A Grateful Heart: Blessings for the Evening Meal from Buddha to the Beatles*, sits on the dinner table. "We didn't have this at the time that she was ill," Elena said. Every night before supper, we would say a blessing by Thoreau. 'For each new morning with its light, for rest and shelter of the night, for health and food for love and friends, we are thankful.' "

"We're not religious, but this was our way of just appreciating that we had a lot. And Liza and her sister Molly altered it to say, "We are *sometimes* thankful," as she was getting more ill, because she was sometimes not feeling very thankful at all. And then after she died we really couldn't bear to say it. So this book was our replacement. And on her memorial days—on her birthday, on her death day—we say the old blessing."

On the walls of the room where we meet hang two large photo montages portraying Liza in all stages of her life and illness: sleeping newborn; grinning baby; delighted toddler; newly diagnosed at age four; in remission with short hair; serenely looking up from a secret project she's working on; bald and bloated, going through another round of chemo; very sick, yet proudly posing with her carefully arranged collection of fifty-six cows; and bedecked in her mother's wedding dress. At the time this latter photo was taken, Liza was in remission and a cure was still hoped for. Then, the photo merely captured a moment of dress-up. Now it is particularly cherished as the only vision Elena will ever have of her daughter Liza in a wedding dress.

The montages were originally made as "storyboards" for Liza's memorial service so that people who did not know her could get a sense of who she was. "Too few people ever got to know her. We wanted her life to be present for people who came out of respect for us but didn't know her," explained Elena. The photos are not in chronological order; they do not document the progression of Liza's illness. Rather, photos from different times of her life are mixed together to give viewers a gestalt of Liza's life. The montages seem to be a physical representation of the way memories of Liza, from all stages of her life, are mixed together in the minds of her family.

Liza first started thinking about dying when she was four and a half. She told her parents she did not want to die because she did not want to be apart from them. This theme of not wanting to be alone shaped her dying. Her parents were open with her throughout all the phases of her illness and dying. They understood her as a very perceptive and direct child who needed to know things as they were. One Friday in the hospital when she had relapsed again, Liza asked if she was going to die from her leukemia. Elena acknowledged the reality of what Liza sensed. That very night she detailed for her mother exactly how she wanted to die. Like people with far more experience to draw upon, Liza designed a death that represented her life. She was ushered out of this life, just as she had been ushered into it, embraced by her family.

"I KNOW HOW I WANT TO DIE"
—Told by Elena Lister

When Liza was admitted into the hospital for pain control, we knew there was nothing else they could offer her. We were awaiting the biopsy results. Both Phil and myself always knew when it was going to be bad news. Before the diagnosis came, we knew. So we had this feeling that it was going to be our worst fear. And her bone marrow transplant doctor came into her room and told her that the leukemia was back. And I was surprised Lizie didn't ask anything at that point. She nodded. I saw that she took it in.

It was my turn to stay with her in the hospital that night. Phil and I took turns. We always watched a lot of Nickelodeon in the evening and I think probably we had rented a movie. And then we were getting ready for bed and were in the bathroom, and she was brushing her teeth and doing a last potty stop. I think I actually was kneeling down next to her helping her with her clothes because her skin was very sensitive.

And that's when she said, "Am I always going to have my leukemia?"

I remember thinking, "Okay, here we go."

She must have been sitting and working though this that afternoon.

I said, "Yeah, we think so."

Then she said, "Am I gonna die from my leukemia?"

I said, "Yeah, we think so."

And then she said, "Am I gonna die soon?"

And I said, "We don't know when."

She said, "Well, will I get to be a teenager?"

I said, "I don't think so."

"Will I get to be a mommy?"

"I don't think so."

That broke my heart because she would have been a great mom.

"Will I get to have my cow?" Liza wanted a live cow in our New York City apartment.

At each of these questions I said, "I don't think so."

At that point I was down on my knees. We were eye to eye and she was leaning on my shoulder and I was holding her, chest to chest. She paused for a minute and was taking it all in.

And then she said, "I know how I want to die."

It just totally blew me away. My guess is that she'd thought about it before, actually. We'd had one or two other conversations about dying, but I think she must have been doing a lot more thinking than she told us about.

"I want to die on your lap. I want to have my lullaby tape on."

Then she said, "I want you to die with me."

I remember thinking at the time, "I think I will."

I could tell she was really picturing this scene because she immediately said, "No, no, no, no. I want you to die right *after* me. I want you to die right after me so you can be with me when I die."

So she really was imagining the scene. She wanted me to be intact, able to be a giving presence while she actually died; then I'd follow her. When she was four and a half she said she didn't want to die because she didn't want to be alone. And, I mean, who does? It's the ultimate aloneness. So I think that was just in keeping with the same line of thinking. So she set a stage. Later on there were elaborations: "I want to die at home. What will dying be like? How will I know when I'm actually dying?"

Her lullaby tape was called "Till Their Eyes Shine." It's a wonderful collection of lullabies from people like Carole King and James Taylor. She listened to it from early infancy. At the hospital she always wanted it on at bedtime. We'd put it on and she would quietly go to sleep. So it was a major comfort to her, and we never went to the hospital without her tape recorder and that tape. Eventually it got worn out from listening to it so much. We went on this mad scramble to find it again, which was not easy at all. After that we taped a few copies of it. So for Liza, the tape had some elemental connection to us and comfort and safety.

That night, after our conversation in the bathroom, she wanted to sleep on me. And I remember feeling her heart beating against me, and feeling like, "I want to make this moment indelibly imprinted on my mind because I'm not going to have this." Her back was to my chest, and I have a vague recollection of a conversation. Lights out in the room, her lying on me and her saying, "So will you die with me?"

That was Liza. I think other kids might have just let it go. And I don't think I ever said "no." I said, "A part of me is going to die with you, and a part of you is going to stay alive with me for always and forever."

Then she asked me if you can talk to people after they've died.

I said, "No, not in the way we do now but kind of with our hearts." I told her that sometimes I think about Grandpa and imagine what he might say to something I've thought and that, in a way, that's a kind of talking and that I would do that with her as well. That seemed to comfort her a great deal. So there was a continuing image of me living on past her to do that.

It was relatively easy to say these things to her because Lizie was so centering. She was a very easy kid to help. She was just so receptive and somehow she made your own heart more available to you because she was so present.

There was another time when we were in the hospital. She was not yet terminal at all. We were post–bone marrow transplant. She was having all sorts of problems, but we were still potentially going for a cure. Her nurse came in and was hanging an antibiotic bag and she said, "I wanna tell you something when Ann leaves."

So I said, "Okay."

And again it was just before bed—that's when everything comes up. My father had died right before her bone marrow transplant in September. And this conversation took place the next March or April, so she had time to think about it. When my father died there were a lot of obituaries in the newspapers. She said, "Do you remember when Grandpa died there were all those notices in the paper? I don't want that when I die."

I said, "Okay. How come?"

She said, "Well for people like"—and she mentioned a couple and their two kids who we're very close with—"I want you to tell them yourself. And then I want them to be able to tell"—and she mentioned the two kids. "Because," she said, "I don't think any-body should hear about that except from their parents." She said, "Dying is private. You should tell the people who need to know, and they should tell their children because it's too much for a child to hear when it's not from their parents." I was just so blown away that she was thinking about these kids' feelings.

I remember these conversations in part because they were life-determining conversations but also because we kept a journal. We wrote down everything that happened from the beginning. It was a way that Phil and I communicated because we would sometimes not see each other for days since we alternated shifts staying in the hospital with Liza. We would write down medical information in the book. Lizie's book, with her tape recorder and her cows, always went to every hospitalization. She would go to sleep and I would write down what happened. I wrote partly because I guess I was aware, even from the beginning, that one day we might not have her to remember with, and partly because it's always been therapeutic for me to write. So writing it helped me process it.

The death scene that Liza envisioned came up several times after she first described it. We had many conversations about dying between the time she was diagnosed as terminal and her death ten weeks later. I asked her what she thought happened after she died, and she thought that she would be with her grandpa and other children who had died of her disease, in particular. She thought there was a leukemia ward in heaven, I think.

And in those conversations she would say, "I want you to make sure that I'm at home when I die." We had a gray couch at the time, and I even think she said, "I want to be on the gray couch. And I want to be on your *lap*. I want to be *on* your lap."

From the moment of terminal diagnosis to her death, Lizie got more and more physically attached to me. We thought of it almost as crawling back into the womb. She would spend the evening hours just sitting on my lap watching TV. She wanted me under and around her at all times. She would take naps on me. I remember trying to carefully slide out from under her to go to the bathroom when she was sleeping.

And I was terrified that I wouldn't be there when she died or that she wouldn't be on my lap when she died. I remember thinking, "What if I'm in the bathroom?" Hospice was actually wonderful for that because they made it very clear to me that I would do what I could and that if she died not on my lap it was because that's when it had to happen. The implication was that people do have some control over the actual moment of their death, and that if she did indeed die when I was not underneath her, then that was a self-determined event. That notion was tremendously relieving to me.

About a week before she died Phil and I were on our way to our weekly meeting with our hospice counselor outside of the house. And Liza said to me, "Mommy, don't go. I don't want you to go."

She'd never really said that. She wasn't clingy. Even though she needed to be on me, she accepted that she would do that when I was there. She didn't try to inhibit me from doing other things. I asked her why and she said, "I just don't feel right."

I missed that appointment and I sat with her on my lap in what we later understood really was a dress rehearsal for her death. I don't know whether she was near it at that point. She did not talk. She just sat on my lap. I think that was some near-death moment. She had to be on my lap. And then she kind of rallied a little bit.

To Get to Be Six

We had an oncologist who was not comfortable facing Liza's terminal condition with her and did not understand that Liza was a "need to know" kind of person. Although we had told Liza that she was dying, he continued to speak to her as though she were not necessarily terminal. The mixed messages made her anxious. We scheduled a meeting with him so she could ask him questions. We listened as she narrowed her window of remaining life to a smaller and smaller future. "Will I get to be seven? Will I live to be six?" We didn't prompt these questions. They were totally from her.

And he looked like, "Oh my God. I can't believe I have to

answer this," and then answered her. He told her that she would not live until her seventh birthday and that he hoped she would live until her sixth. He told her that we would know when the day was soon and that he would tell her when her time was near. That conversation was reassuring for Liza. She knew the truth, she knew that we knew it, and she needed to know that we could all know it together. After that talk Liza grew less anxious. When she asked the oncologist, "Will I live to my sixth birthday?" and he said "I hope so," that became her goal: to get to be six.

Liza called her sixth birthday her "happy sad birthday." When people wanted to sing "Happy Birthday," she sang "Happy sad birthday to me." We had a birthday party, which she helped plan. We invited family and some of our friends and two friends of hers from school who ended up canceling the morning of the party. I think their parents just freaked out. One of the clown care unit doctors, Dr. Bobo, who Liza really liked, came as the entertainment.

Liza and I made two cakes. We always make the cakes and the kids always decorate them. We put a big cloth on the table and put out sprinkles and icing pens, and they can go to town. And Lizie sat and got into one of her things—this was a creation on her part. She did this whole thing where she wrote each of our initials: E for me, P for Phil, M for her sister, Molly, C for Cleveth her baby-sitter, O for her grandmother, and L for herself. And she organized us around her and put little nonpareils around each initial.

And there was an exit place for her in this arrangement. There was a story of her moving forward. The way she described it, the L was able to travel out. There was some pathway where she's surrounded by us but able to go. I understood that she was talking about being surrounded by us but dying. I almost didn't want to eat the cake because it was a story about her. So she really worked on this cake the whole night before.

We had the party, and she had maybe one bite of cake and was vomiting. She just couldn't enjoy it. And the clown was too much; she couldn't take the stimulation. She didn't want everybody to leave, but she couldn't do anything. It was very painful. It was the let-down of the other kids not coming and the knowledge that clearly this was her last birthday. She was wanting to celebrate but also sensed how bizarre it was to celebrate at that point. It was just a very painful day. I remember after people left we felt mostly relieved—she had made it to the birthday, she'd made it to the party.

She died twelve days after her sixth birthday. She had been determined to live through her sixth birthday, and her oncologist has said to us that she did that by pure spit and vim. It was just pure determination because she really was just riddled with leukemia and had no white cells left. But she wanted to make it to her birthday. After that there was a sharp decline. She'd made it to the point that she'd promised herself. And my understanding from hospice is that this is not uncommon, that people will pick a date and get themselves there and then begin to fail after that.

Three or four days after her birthday I was giving her a sponge bath. She couldn't have real baths because of all the various tubing. I loved giving her those baths because it was a very body-contact time and for all those months in the bone marrow transplant unit we weren't allowed to have contact. And she felt so delicious.

And she said to me, "Mommy I'm tired. I'm so, so tired."

And I thought, "Okay, here's my moment; she's giving me an entree to tell her it's okay to let go."

I knew that she needed that, and I thank hospice for helping us understand that. Because it was so painful for me to give her permission to go, that I don't know if I could have said it if I didn't understand how important it was to her to do that.

And that's when I told her, "I know you have to die, and I know you don't want to, and I don't want you to. But when you are so, so tired that's okay. I will be okay because, and only because, I will always have you in my heart." And I pointed to my chest.

She said, "Mommy that's not your heart, that's your breast."

Here this kid is *dying*, and she's joking with me. I said, "Okay so it's a little over there, but it's somewhere in that vicinity."

And then she said, "What's going to happen when you die?" Meaning, if I held her in my heart and I died what would happen to her. I said, "Then Molly will hold both of us, and if she has children, they will hold all of us. And it goes on and on and on and on."

After that, she basically stopped fighting. We think of that as the pivotal moment that she really needed to just know from us that she could let go and that we would be okay.

The Death She Wanted

Liza died on a Sunday morning at around ten o'clock in the morning. The previous Friday was Molly's ninth birthday. Saturday was Molly's birthday party. It was a bowling party. I thought that Lizie was dying, but we had twenty-five kids coming to this party. So Phil and Molly went to the party and Lizie sat in my lap really just clutching me. She didn't want to move; she didn't want the TV on; she didn't want books. She just sat. I felt like she was trying to hold on until they came back from the party. I also think that she didn't want to die on Molly's birthday party day. I think she didn't want to ruin Molly's birthday. That may seem impossible, but if you knew Lizie I think you would see that it's possible that she would be thoughtful about the impact it would have on Molly to die on her birthday party day.

They came home from the party. The rest of that evening unfolded with Lizie retching, which is really just an awful thing but is a common terminal sign. She was very uncomfortable . . . flushed . . . having a difficult time breathing. We called the pain doctor, who determined that she would come over as soon as she could. Clearly, something was dramatically wrong and we knew that we weren't going to rush her to the hospital and that basically this was it. Molly was very dejected, sort of understanding that this was happening, and not having had a single moment with me the whole day of her birthday or birthday party. Molly went up to bed at around ten o'clock, and Phil and I just figured, "We're gonna wait this out as long as it takes."

Lizie, by the way, after she asked for her lullaby tape to be playing when she died, for the next ten weeks she refused to listen to it. That night she said, "I want my lullaby tape on." She said that before anybody said anything to her about the fact that she was actually dying. And we just put it in; we didn't announce that as significant. Then she wanted to watch *I Love Lucy*, which was one of her favorite shows. She was Lucy-like. She was really a ham. But she really couldn't tolerate the stimuli of the television. That was when the pain doctor came, gave her a lot of morphine, tried to get her to stop retching, and told us that she felt this was basically it— a matter of who knows how long—she could slip into a coma and actually go for a while or she would die imminently.

Phil went up to get Molly because we thought it might be imminent. When he brought her back down, Lizie said to Molly, "Molly, it's my time to die— they tell me it's my time to die and I want you to know that I love you."

It was so clear and so powerful and so much a determined effort—with the few words Lizie could get out she wanted to tell her sister this. It was really clear that she somehow knew that Molly needed this to carry with her through life. I think she was really taking care of Molly.

Lizie was very controlling, lest you forget. And to Phil's and Molly's heartbreak that night that she was dying, she would not let anybody else hold her. I think she was just scared that if she went to somebody else she might not die on me—maybe she didn't realize she could control it as much as she could. So the others huddled around the unity of Lizie and me but were not able to hold her, which they had such a hunger to do.

Lizie had called for our baby-sitter who'd been with us since Molly was born. She and Lizie had the same birthday, and "Liza" happened to also be the name of the baby-sitter's mother-figure. So they were sort of cosmically connected from the beginning. And Lizie called her in Brooklyn and said, "You must come. I'm dying." This was Saturday night, and Cleveth, our baby-sitter, was at her own birthday party but she came in anyway.

So Lizie sort of orchestrated. She had Cleveth there, she had my mother-in-law there. And then she said to me, "There's something I want to tell you but I can't do it."

And I remember Phil and I saying to her, "Don't worry, we know it." Because I thought that she was trying to do for us what she had done for Molly. But she was spent, she just couldn't do it anymore. I remember feeling at the moment that we absolutely didn't want her to feel like she had let us down and not left us with anything. But afterward I hungered to know what she was going to say. I want to have what we want Molly to have—those last final words.

Anyway, at one point I left to go to the bathroom and she let Phil hold her. When I came back she asked me to pick her up and hold her. And I picked her up. She was sort of chest to chest with me. And I tell you it's the weirdest thing. I don't believe in an afterlife, but she looked at the upper corner of the living room and seemed to sort of get calm and was breathing easier, and then she said, "Now ready."

Phil and I said, "Did she really do that?"

Everyone who was in the room said, "Yes, she did." Then she went into a coma, and she died about eight hours later.

She waited for me to come back from the bathroom and pick her up and then she said, "Now ready." So maybe she had a sense that she had everybody assembled, she'd done the good deed for Molly, and Molly's birthday party day was over. She knew it was already the next day, she knew it was like two o'clock in the morning, when she became comatose.

So she went into a coma—although she didn't die,—with her head resting on my shoulder. But I felt that was close to being on my lap. And then, as she lay comatose, we passed her around. Phil held her and snuggled with her and Molly held her. We have pictures of Lizie comatose on Molly's lap. My mother-in-law held her and all the people who wanted contact held her. Then we took her upstairs to our bedroom. We knew that we needed to lie down, and we all wanted to be around her. The best way to all be around her was to go on our bed. We also felt we did not know how long this was going to take. She could be in a coma for weeks, so we had to find some way to live with this. Molly, Phil, and I carried her upstairs. We laid her on her back, propped up on pillows, with us under her and around her. Molly was at her feet when she actually died. She was in my arms with Phil's arm basically around her when she took her last breaths. Terminal breathing has a certain rhythm. It's hnn hhh, hnn hhh. I can still hear it so easily. It's very vivid in my head. We were listening and then her breaths grew farther and farther spaced apart.

Something that came up in the hospice meetings before she died was that obviously this scene where she's on my lap and we're all together was a dream scene. We were just lucky it turned out that way. It could have been that she would have had *grand mal* seizures, she could have had a stroke, she could have gone into a coma, not on my lap, never come out of it, and lived like that for two months. So we were just very lucky that it happened the way it did. And I think the pain and palliative care doctor helped a lot by making sure that she was adequately medicated toward the end. I don't know if it stopped seizures, but I just think she escorted Lizie medically through it. Lizie really did have the death she wanted. It was just such a blessing.

Remembering Liza

A year after Liza died, we held a memorial service in her honor. A family friend who had played the guitar at all of Liza's and Molly's birthday parties performed a song from Liza's lullaby tape: Carole King's "What Would I Do if I Didn't Have You to Wake Up to Each Day?" Then we invited our dearest friends over to all partake in this bizarre meal made up of Liza's favorite foods: Mike and Ike candies, five-flavor Lifesavers, chocolate mint hard candies, beefsteak tomatoes, pizza cut into quarter slices. It was really a riot.

On her birthdays we let go of a helium balloon, usually something Disney. At ten she might have been tired of Disney, but at six she was still completely immersed in it. Also, the Starlight Foundation had asked her what she wanted, and she said a trip to Disney World. But she was never well enough to go; she never got to do that trip. So we send up a Disney balloon. Molly and I always do it. Phil actually doesn't. It's not his thing. We go to a playground that Lizie loved. I have a cherished memory of Lizie in that park. She's terminally ill, and she's riding her bicycle. She has the tubing coming out of her chest into a bag, and I'm holding the bag, running behind her so that the tubing doesn't fly out of her chest. She's biking—terminally ill. That park was a place we always went, so we go to the park and let the balloons go from there. Molly and I always get one for each of us.

The first year Molly wanted the two of us to write something to Lizie on it. She wrote a note telling Lizie that a new brother was coming—I was pregnant at that time—that she knew how Lizie would have loved this little brother, and that she missed her a lot. It was just really splendid. I wrote that this was a day when I remembered her a lot and that I remembered her every day anyway. We taped the notes to the ribbons attached to the balloons.

We let go of them and sent them up. Mine went off, but Molly's got caught in a tree. I thought, "Oh no, I don't want this to be bad for her."

The wind was blowing. She had folded her note over, and the wind just sort of blew it open. I said, "It's being read. It doesn't matter that it got caught—look, we can see that the card's been opened." And Molly was relieved.

We've done that every year on her birthday. Initially we also did it on her half-birthday, but now we've stopped doing that. Her half-birthdays became very important when she was ill. We celebrated half-birthdays, which we had never done before, partly in recognition on some level that we did not know what her next birthday would bring, but also because on her fourth birthday she was so ill, not yet diagnosed. On her fifth birthday she had just relapsed. So no birthday was untainted, and half-birthdays became important.

This year, the fourth year of Lizie's birthday and death date, which are twelve days apart, Molly didn't want to go to the park. I felt I still wanted to do it. Phil and our son, Sol, came with me. And I got Sol a balloon.

I was amazed, because kids don't let go of balloons easily. If Sol gets one, he holds on very tightly and if it bursts he gets very upset. I told him in advance that this was a balloon we were going to have to let go, so if he didn't want to get one that was okay, but if he got it he had to let it go. It was a gift for his sister Liza. To my amazement, he embraced the experience and let it go. "Bye-bye balloon. Happy birthday Liza. Happy birthday Liza."

The Last Passage

After extensive research on the Huichol Indians, anthropologist Barbara Myerhoff turned to the study of elderly Jews. She explained her decision thus, "However much I learned from [the study of the Indians] was limited by the fact that I would never really be a Huichol Indian. But I *would* be a little old Jewish lady." Tragically, Barbara never did become an old Jewish lady. She died at the age of fifty but she left behind a magnificent book, *Number Our Days,* chronicling the lives of elderly men and women at a senior center in Venice, California. Among them was Jacob Koved, who died on his ninety-fifth birthday, but who struggled poetically with the angel of death. Critically ill for months before his birthday, yet determined to celebrate it, he designed his life until the very end. Ingeniously, he found a symbolic way to number his days to the age of one hundred.

In *The Last Passage: Recovering a Death of Our Own,* Donald Heinz writes of the importance of constructing our life stories, "of turning our lives into larger myths that can bear the weight of significant meaning." He cites the death of Jacob Koved as an example of a "successfully staged last chapter." In Jacob's story, "death was transformed from an antagonist to a partner. In making his death a mythic and symbolic drama, Jacob transcended it . . . His [final birthday] party was a successful ritual, his storied dying an act of poetry and mythmaking."

UNTIL I AM ONE HUNDRED
—*Written by Barbara Myerhoff*

[On the day of Jacob Koved's ninety-fifth birthday] the weather was exceptionally fair and celebrants came streaming toward the Israel Levin Senior Center on the boardwalk in Venice Beach, California, several hours too early. That the day was set apart was clear from people's appearance: the women in white gloves holding perfectly preserved purses from other decades, wearing symbolic jewelry, often expensive gifts from their children—golden medallions bearing grandchildren's names, "Tree of Life" necklaces studded with real pearls, Stars of David, and the golden letters "Chai," Hebrew for life and luck ... Glowing haloes from scarves and bright hats colored the women's expectant faces. Men wore tidy suits polished with use, over frayed, starched shirts.

The Center hall was festively decorated, and people were seated formally. At the head table was the Koved family, and around it, the dignitaries. Jacob, it was learned, was behind the curtain of the little stage, receiving oxygen, and so the ceremony was delayed for about half an hour. At last he came out to applause and took his seat. Jacob's son Sam was the master of ceremonies. Music called the assembly to order and people were greeted with "Shalom," Hebrew for peace. Jacob was presented as the guest of honor, followed by introductions, referring first to the whole Koved family as *mishpocheh* (family), then extending the term to include all those assembled; all present were an extended family. Each member of the Koved family was named, including the absent ones, along with their profession, academic titles, and degrees, generation by generation. Sam greeted the assembly on behalf of "Pa, his children, his children's children, and even their children." The *broche* (blessing) in Hebrew was followed by the traditional Jewish toast, "*L'chayim,*" to health and life.

Then Sam set out the order of events in detail, including a specification of when Jacob's gift to the center would be described (during his speech), when dessert would be served (with speeches), and when the cake would be served (after speeches).

The meal went smoothly, and no unusual developments were evident to the assembly, but privately, when Moshe came over to congratulate him, Jacob whispered that he wished people would hurry and eat; "*Malakh-hamoves* [the angel of death; God's messenger] is near and hasn't given me much time," he said.

As dessert was about to be served, Sam took the microphone and began his speech, in which he recounted some biographical details of Jacob's life and certain cherished characteristics. He emphasized his father's idealism and social activism in the Old Country and in America and spoke at some length about the courtship and marriage of their parents. Though their mother had died twenty-four years ago, she remained a strong influence in keeping the family together. . . .

During Sam's speech, Jacob was again taken backstage to receive oxygen. People were restive and worried, but Sam assured them that Jacob would soon return and the program would continue. Eventually Jacob took his seat, leaning over to tell one of the young people in English, and Moshe in Yiddish, that he had little time and wished they would hurry to his part of the program, for now he said, "*Ich reingle sich mutten Malakh-hamoves* [I am wrestling with the Angel of Death]."

The progression was interrupted briefly when his sons recognized Jacob's difficulty breathing and gave him oxygen at his seat . . . At last the sign was given that Jacob was ready. Abe announced the revised sequence of events: Jacob's speech in Yiddish, then in English, then dignitaries' speeches, then the cake. Jacob remained seated but began his speech vigorously. It was characteristic that Jacob's Yiddish was free of anglicized words, distinctly articulated and syntactically correct; this respect for the language was understood by the old people to bespeak Jacob's respect for his heritage.

After a few sentences he faltered, slowed, and finished word by word. Here are selections from his speech in translation:

Dear friends: every other year I have had something significant to say, some meaningful message when we came together for this *yontif* (holiday). But this year, I don't have an important message. I don't have the strength . . . It is very hard for me to accept the idea that I am played out. . . . Nature has a good way of expressing herself when bringing humanity to the end of its years, but when it touches you personally it is hard to comprehend . . . I do have a wish for today. . . . It is this: that my last five years, until I am one hundred, my birthday will be celebrated here with you. . . . whether I am here or not. It will be an opportunity for the members of my beloved Center to be together for a *simcha* (happy occasion) and at the same time raise money for our beleaguered Israel."

The message was powerful in its stated and unstated content—made even more so by the dramatic circumstances in which it was delivered. Jacob's passion to be heard and to complete his purpose was perhaps the strongest communication. He was demonstrating what he had told me in an earlier interview, that he sustained himself as an autonomous, lucid person, using thinking, speaking, and writing as his shields against dissolution and despair.

Jacob finished amid great applause. His and the audience's relief were apparent. He sat quietly in his place at the table, folded his hands, and rested. Just as Sam began to read his father's speech in English, Jacob's head fell forward gently, then back, and his mouth opened slightly. Oxygen was administered within the surrounding circle of his sons as Abe took the microphone and asked for calm and quiet. After a few moments, his sons lifted Jacob, still seated in his chair, and carried him behind the curtain, accompanied by Moshe, Abe, and the rabbi.

Soon Abe returned and reassured the hushed assembly that a rescue unit had been called, that everything possible was being done, and that Jacob wanted people to finish their dessert:

"Be assured that Jacob knew the peril of coming today. All we can do is pray. He's in the hands of God. His sons are with him. He most of all wanted to be here. Remember his dignity and yours and let him be an example. You must eat your dessert. You must, we must all, continue. We go on living. Now your dessert will be served."

People ate quietly. Regularly Abe came to the front to reassure them, with special firmness when the fire department siren was heard outside. He explained at length all the steps that were being taken to save Jacob, and concluded.

"He's very delicate. Your cooperation is very beautiful. Jacob wants us to continue. You heard his speech. We all have a date to keep. Out of love and respect for Jacob we will be meeting here for the next five years on his birthday. We will be here, you will be here, whether to celebrate with him or commemorate him. They are taking Jacob away now. The hospital will telephone us, and we will tell you how he is doing."

People complied and continued eating. There were many who quietly spoke their certainty that Jacob was dead and had died in their midst. The conviction was strongest among those few who noticed that after the rabbi and Moshe left Jacob behind the curtain, they went to the bathroom before returning to their seats. Perhaps it was only hygiene, they said, but it was also known that religious Jews are enjoined to wash their hands after contact with the dead. Hence, the gesture was read as portentous.

The room was alive with quiet remarks:

"He's gone. That was how he wanted it. He said what he had to say and he finished."

"It was a beautiful life, a beautiful death."

"There's a saying, when the fig is plucked in due time, it's good for the fig and good for the tree."

"Did you see how they carried him out? Like Elijah, he died in his chair. Like a bridegroom."

"He died like a *tzaddik* (holy man)."

"Moses also died on his birthday, in the month of Nisan. . . ."

With great difficulty, Abe regained control of the people, reminding them sternly that the ceremony had not concluded. There remained one dignitary who had not yet spoken. This, Abe pointed out, was insulting to the group he represented.

Abe was improvising here, no longer able to utilize the guidelines of the birthday metaphor. The ceremony threatened to break apart. In actuality, Abe was worried about letting people go home without knowing Jacob's fate. It would be difficult for him to handle their anxieties in the next few days if they were left in suspense. And no one wanted to leave. The circumstances clearly called for some closure, some provision of order. The last dignitary began to talk while Abe was wondering what to do next. Then the phone rang and everyone was quite still. Uncertainly the speaker persisted, though no one was listening. Abe came forward and announced what everyone already knew.

"God in his wisdom has taken Jacob away from us, in His mystery He has taken him. So you must understand that God permitted Jacob to live ninety-five years and to have one of his most beautiful moments here this afternoon. You heard his last words. We will charter a bus and go together to his funeral. He gave you his last breath. I will ask the rabbi to lead us in a prayer as we stand in solemn tribute to Jacob."

Home Altars

Altars are places where contact can be made between this world and the other; they are places where relationships with the divine or with the dead can be maintained through ritual activity. In some Catholic and Buddhist traditions, family members create home altars to honor and interact with their ancestors. On the Mexican Day of the Dead, for example, when the spirits of the dead are believed to return annually to visit their families, the spirits are welcomed with earthly pleasures like food, drink, and cigarettes, which are set out for them on an altar or *ofrenda*. Some people who were raised in religions that do not include the tradition of home altars have adapted it as a means of ongoing commemoration of and communication with their dead. They have transformed a communal rite into a personal one. Marlene Lortev Terwilliger conceives of altars as sacred places that allow her to "ritualize feeling." Her sister's death from lung cancer at the age of fifty-two inspired her to make a commemorative altar replete with personal symbolism.

HOUSE OF CARDS

—Told by Marlene Lortev Terwilliger

I knew that I could not return to "normal" existence without finding a formal or ritual way of maintaining my sister's presence in my life. What got me started was a fantasy that we'd shared—when we were old we'd live together in a little house by the sea. We'd pick a place where there was a library or a bookstore in town and a cafe. The rest would be up to us.

The altar took shape slowly. I knew from the start that the foundation would be a bed of sand. I discovered a marvelous deck of *Alice in Wonderland* cards and out of them constructed our house. It was perfect—a story from our childhood and a link to our father, who'd been great at amusing us with his talent for building elaborate structures with cards.

Once the house was built I decided we'd occupy it in the form of Matisse women, odalisques who have always touched me and felt "true" to us. I found a cafe table and chairs and a coffee pot and cups. The next big challenge was the candles and flowers. I wanted a four-candle holder for the four seasons, but none that I saw was right. Finally, I found the perfect one, with mermaids (who'd swim in our sea). It was only for three candles, but that turned out fine because I found a separate holder that would be right for the candle of each season. Thus the changing of the candles, a different color for each season, became an important ritual element . . . I had a Lucite box made and filled it with sand from the beach. I gathered pine cones, shells, stones at the beach, and bought little objects I thought we'd have or would be there—a typewriter, a writing pad and pencil, a fish, a bird. Flowers were hard to come by, but finally I found some simple wooden Balinese ones I knew were right. I called the altar "We Share the Moon," a translation of the Chinese characters on the card in the center of the altar. On the backside of the card there is a poem—"I look up at the moon/And my heart feels you/ Although a thousand miles away/ Watching this same moon."

The altar is very "alive" for me. It continues to evolve and change as I add new objects, things Barbara might have wanted to include in our world, such as a pail and shovel for kids who might be at the beach or our own grandchildren when they visited. Recently I added a little altar within the altar—and a skeletal bone I found on the beach.

In addition to letting the altar change as I find new objects for it, I also spend time "keeping it up," readjusting the house, clearing sand from the steps, brushing off the typewriter. I love doing these domestic chores about the altar, but mainly I love and need the rituals. Each solstice and on my sister's birthday I perform a ritual. I buy fresh seasonal flowers, surround the altar with her pictures, change and light the candles, burn incense. I play music softly, meditate, speak to her, dance, or cry . . . The altar is a memorial, a way of honoring my sister, of keeping her with me in my life forever. It is a way to express my grief and my love.

A Prom and a Yearbook

The prom is an American rite of passage that represents both the culmination of, and the end to, carefree adolescence. On one festive day at the AIDS Day Treatment Program in Chelsea, New York, this rite was transformed into an end-of-life ritual. When Laura, a client with AIDS, lamented that she had never had a prom, her community at the Program came together to plan the occasion and were further inspired to compile a yearbook as well. Many of those at the Program had experienced loss of health; some had lost rights to their children; some had lost friends; and some were about to lose their lives. They could do nothing about these losses. But Laura's sense of loss over her missed prom experience was something that could be addressed. Her wish inspired an outrageously creative gala, a community project that had a restorative effect on many of the participants. And the yearbook, with its inventive pictures and listing of people's nicknames, favorite activities, and ambitions, became a remarkable collective life review project.

For twelve years, Lila Zeiger, who tells the story, has been on the staff of the AIDS Day Treatment Program. As a writer, she helps clients express their pain and leave a legacy. But as she says, the Program is "a place where people are stopped in their tracks, where we appreciate the irony that, for many, their diagnosis signaled a poignant desire to break out of self-destructive patterns and live fully. Seeing those we love dying among us every day, the very idea of mourning becomes so intense—and so intolerable—that we must almost seem to reject it. Our emphasis is indeed on living, on using all of our abilities and resources to experience as much fulfillment and joy as we can. Therefore, I am part archivist, part tummler"—referring to the social director/comedians who entertained at Jewish resorts in the Catskills. "An important facet of our program is to relieve the stress we face each day—to do the unexpected, the unconventional, and to have fun!"

"I use the word fun in the most serious way," she says. "When people hear where I work, they often make the assumption that I am a combination of Mother Teresa and Lady Bountiful. While I do not deny the difficulty and the pain, I hasten to explain how lucky I am to have found this place—and this work, which enriches me more than anything I have ever done. How do all of us at the Program live with the loss of so many people whom we have known and cared for and loved? For me, by now, it must be close to a thousand too-early deaths. We know that life is finite, but this modern plague, of which we still understand so little, has been marked by a poignant variety of endings: the handsome face covered with Karposi's Sarcoma lesions, the robust frame reduced by wasting, the brilliant brain dimmed by dementia."

"Some of us," she says, "know the guilt of the bystander, the chasm that separates us from those we love when we ourselves do not have the virus, the uneasiness of using that 'we.' But from day to day, from unpredictable minute to minute, our lives are filled with comraderie and courage, with the sense that we are together, that we are living fully. And yes, that we must give ourselves the right to have pleasure, to have fun."

"WHEN THIS YOU SEE, REMEMBER ME"
—Written by Lila Zeiger
(Names have been changed to protect privacy.)

It all started one spring morning in 1998, when Laura, a client at the AIDS Day Treatment Program where I work, exclaimed, almost out of the blue, "I never had a prom!" Our Laura, who struggled every day with her obesity and with her addiction to drugs, which could make her nod off into her cereal many mornings. Laura, who cried with the frustration of not being able to mother her beloved daughter or prevent her own mother from taking over her life when she herself could not function. Why never having had a prom, of all the many severe deprivations in her life, should suddenly emerge so painfully was not for us to ask. We knew only that the month of May had come once more, and with it a romantic possibility entirely within our reach: Laura and the other women (and men, too, if they chose!) enveloped in various shades of bright satin, gyrating around the dance floor to the disco beat of a live band and also our favorite and very lively D.J. The Day Room would be transformed into a kind of night garden in the Alhambra, with murals we would paint to disguise the fact that the walls—and ceiling, too—were coming down at any moment.

Our AIDS Day Treatment Program, the first of its kind in the United States, had been in existence for almost ten years then, and there was almost nothing our intrepid staff would not try to improve the lives of our "clients" (the best word, that) who were joined together as a community from 8:30 to 4:00 each day by virtue of a random "virus" (again, probably the best word).

We began planning for a prom date of Thursday, May 28. The party would begin at 11:00 A.M. and end at 7:00 P.M.—a necessary reversal of the usual hours. We even dared to call it the Last Dance Prom (a sensitive choice, that word "last"!) because our building was being gutted to become a luxury rental and we knew we'd never have another dance at this location. It would serve as a kind of graduation, really. Before I knew it, I said, "Then we've got to have a yearbook!" As it turned out, I was to regret that remark for the next four months!

Despite the fact that my title was "Creative Writing Specialist," an elegant description not of my choosing, the truth was that I didn't know precisely what a yearbook was, never having had one myself—or a prom either, for that matter. I envisioned our year-book as a simple handmade booklet, with a layout of words and photos to be duplicated on our Canon copy machine and stapled so that everyone at the prom could get one. But the traditional year-book formats I examined just didn't seem meaningful or applicable to our needs, and, slowly but inexorably, an idea grew, like some out-of-control mutant creature, of a homemade book that would be entirely ours, would include all of us—staff and clients, close to 130 people—with unique, detailed entries to be written by each person, and displaying, two people to a page, our own sense of who we were and what we wished ourselves to be.

Festivities

The prom was a huge success. It went off as planned on May 28. Everyone had received an invitation and a program. We dined, we danced, we flirted, we voted for a king and queen. The invitations wisely advised, "Creative Prom Attire Requested." As the photo montages in the yearbook show, this could be anything from tux to (of course!) drag to striped T-shirt. The staff had collected as many formal costumes as we could to provide for those who might need them. I wore a little constantly-falling-off-the-shoulder number from the free bin at a Vermont thrift store. But Curtis, who was chosen King of the Prom, and who had once worked on a cruise ship, looked elegant in his own tuxedo and tails, his blond tresses flowing as he paraded and even danced, although he had just been hospitalized and was still so seriously ill that he could barely walk. (That is the kind of incredible courage that we are accustomed to seeing all the time.) Robby, the Queen, who frolicked on Curt's arm, really *is* a queen, which made everything more wonderful. A professional female impersonator and talented performer, he (she) was gorgeous in a faux diamond tiara and pearls and had secretly lobbied the other clients to gain well-deserved votes for the King.

For those revelers who weren't lavishly attired, our own artists had painted two wooden panels of a man and woman dressed in utter elegance. They stood side by side against the wall, so that everyone who wished to, kids included, could stick their heads in the holes cut out and be photographed the way you would at a carnival. There were paper corsages in every color of the rainbow. The Class of '98! We had everything we'd been promised—but, of course, no yearbooks. Yet!

The very morning of the prom, some of us attended a memorial downtown for one of the clients, Dev, who had died unexpectedly, although he had had a premonition that he'd never make it to the end of May. When I later returned to the festivities, where people were asking for their yearbooks, all I could do was explain lamely that the project was taking longer than we had thought, but that eventually we would have a yearbook. Then began the weeks and months of making it happen, of discovering how it should be done, how it could be done, with maximum expectation and minimal budget.

Black and White, Not Living Color

Certain things became clear. This book would be totally untraditional. Entries for the staff and clients would be mixed, and there would be no such thing as alphabetical order. People could be creative in choosing their own portraits, from baby pictures to present likenesses. Only two or three clients had actual graduation pictures, some even with mortarboard and gown. Our doctor used his Bar Mitzvah photo; he was dressed in a snazzy tuxedo and frilled shirt.

A few people brought photos taken in uniform when they were in the service. One of our devoted couples used pictures of themselves at confirmation, each holding his prayer book in hand. We collected pictures of people in drag; making fierce muscles; standing among enormous cacti; being decorated with a medal by a father; or posing with Donald Duck at Disneyland. Our acupuncturist, who revealed her obsession with footwear, chose a photo of herself as a toddler caressing her mother's spike-heeled pump. Paul, who had a wicked sense of humor, claimed that his hobby was "long-distance swimming" and found a weird newsprint picture of an obese, hairy swimmer in a scanty bikini, looking rather apprehensive, with little goggles perched on his forehead like a tiny crown.

As soon as we got an entry, it would be typed so that the writer could see it, discuss it—or change it. And there were many changes in all those months that we worked on the yearbook, which was soon approaching eighty pages. People would come into the Program, and people would leave. Couples who had been sure they would last forever were insisting after breaking up that they could not even bear to be together on the same page. Clients would even call from rehab or prison about vitally necessary changes—and I'd make them!

What we did not anticipate was that so few of our clients would have photos to bring in. When you have lived on the margins, in single-room-occupancy conditions, when you have been robbed of your possessions more than once, or when you have been estranged from your family or your homeland, you're not likely to have too many pictures of yourself. Thus it was that we often had to use I.D. cards on the copier, appalled by how poorly they came out. There was no rhyme or reason to how facial tones would reproduce, or how the stamps on the I.D. cards would mar a person's face. In desperation, I sometimes used Wite-Out to alter the skin tones or to make a "necklace" or collar. We had a Polaroid with which we could take pictures of people who had none to bring in, but those usually translated poorly on the page as well. Ned, a Renaissance man who was expert at graphic design (as well as everything else), was invaluable in devising the schematic layout and making guesses as to which tones would come out best. We'd sit with our glue sticks and scissors in the midst of the Day Room, he and I, to make up the first few sample pages that would give everyone an idea of what the book would look like. But even using every setting on the Canon, we could never be sure of the final shots. And the action-filled collages of the prom doings looked totally distorted. Yet, seeing this Rogue's Gallery we often ended up with, or marveling at how some of the pictures looked as if they should be hung in the Wanted section at the post office, these problems somehow became unimportant. We knew who we were, we cared for one another, and all together this way, we made a terrific group, teeming with life!

Success

By the end of September 1998, we were in our beautiful new quarters down the block and celebrating our tenth anniversary with the yearbooks in our hands. Bree had been waiting patiently to get her yearbook. A relatively new client, she had been very shy in the first few months. Childlike in demeanor, her favorite activity was straightening up, sponging the table tops, and being a "good girl" and of service to others. Her sweetness was very real. Although she had little money, she would bring in clothing to donate, as well as workbooks that she had collected in her striving to overcome her own illiteracy. We became close very soon. When I hugged her, I was careful of the sometimes open wounds from the mutilation she inflicted on her arms. She even wrote once, secretly, never to be shared on our Poetry Wall, of the "bad Bree" who cuts herself. One day we cried together when she dictated a letter to me for her son in prison into which she slipped a twenty-dollar bill—all she could afford to send him. I was amazed to realize that she had a grown child, because she looked like a teenage tomboy herself. But at times she would come in to the Program very disinhibited, with her eyes heavily made up to disguise the ravages of heavy drinking or perhaps a beating, the mascara running when she wept at being sent home.

The evening I came back with the yearbooks all packed up and ready for our anniversary celebration the next day, Bree clapped her hands like a kid, laughed, and kissed me. "Tomorrow I'll see my book!" She never made it in the next day. She died that night of an overdose. I didn't want to find out the details. At her memorial, we used her yearbook entry in the little booklet we prepared. Bree, a.k.a. Rugrat. Bree, who lists as one of her hobbies, "doing word puzzles," whose favorite things were "puppies and kittens," who said, with insight, that she was most likely to "be a good listener if people have problems." How I wish she could have seen her book! But there she is, very much a part of it. She stands there beaming, her hands in her pockets, looking really sweet—and really happy.

Celebration

Our first look at the yearbooks helped to mark our passage into a new decade. We autographed each other's books, and we laughed over the entries, which we had never seen before. While we complained about a picture here and there or wished we had said something different, we sensed the uniqueness of this experience. It was a real rite of passage, and we knew that there would never be a book like this again! Everyone had a plain brown envelope in which to take the yearbook home, and very few of them were lost. To this day, people talk about the tenth anniversary, and we still use the yearbook entries for memorials, which are less frequent than they were in the past, but therefore sometimes even more painful. Reading everyone's own words in one book made a lasting impression, and some clients who had never written before began keeping journals and writing about their childhood as a result of those first answers to a list of the questions we gave them about their hobbies and ambitions.

Was it all worth it? Each time we look at the yearbook and see our almost unrecognizable faces and preposterous getups, each time we read the special things we had to say about ourselves, we know how well we have commemorated our existence. We remembered our past and gamely made up for what each of us had lost. We tried to define who and how we were at present. We looked to the future with hope and with humor. What better way to praise our distinct being and our common humanity? What better way to give the finger to time? To death?

Chronicle Of a Death Foretold

When someone dies in a small town or even in a close-knit community in the city, it is customary for the funeral procession to drive by the house of the departed on its way to the cemetery. Sometimes the cavalcade, led by the hearse, drives by several places that were meaningful to the deceased. This takes the deceased and the mourners on a visit to these significant places one last time in a review of, and a tribute to, the person's life. Ilana's grandfather David Chasman served as a cantor in a synagogue in the Boston suburb of Malden, Massachusetts. His funeral procession stopped at each of the four synagogues in Malden and also at the Malden Hebrew School, as his life was devoted to the synagogue and to Jewish education. When the hearse stopped in front of each building, the doors were opened and a designated rabbi chanted the memorial prayer, *El Maleh Rahamim*.

At the funeral of Miguel Pinero, who belonged to a tight-knit community of poets on the Lower East Side of Manhattan, a procession of mourners visited places that Miguel had inhabited. They were on foot, not in cars, and they brought Miguel along not in a hearse, but in a can of ashes. And at each spot along the route, which he had mapped out before his death, they scattered some of his ashes.

This ritual was created out of a collaborative effort between Miguel, when he was alive, and his friends, following his death. Miguel had detailed in verse what was to be done upon his death, and his friends complied with his unconventional request. His poem exuded a contagious energy that gathered the community around him and bound them with each other at the time of his death. Even as his remains were cast to the wind, he was very much a presence, one might even say an active participant at his funeral. As hospice worker Katherine Blossom notes, "People say 'When I die I want this to happen' or 'I want that to happen.' People plan their funerals because they want the time of their death to *mean* them," to signify the essence of who they were on this earth.

SCATTER MY ASHES
—Written by Miguel Algarín

Many years ago, two poets made a promise to each other, and the promise was deceptively simple. One poet promised the other that by the next evening he would come back with a poem that would lay out in detail what was to be done upon his death.

> *Just once before I die*
> *I want to climb up on a*
> *tenement sky*
> *to dream my lungs out till*
> *I cry*
> *then scatter my ashes thru*
> *the Lower East Side.*

So it came to pass that my friend Miguel Pinero would die, on June 17, 1988. When I arrived in New York, I went immediately to the Wollensky Funeral Parlor, where a great poet lay in state. I knew I was to conduct the ceremonies attendant upon a Nuyorican poet (a New York Puerto Rican poet associated with New York's renowned Nuyorican Poets Cafe), which meant that there would be a call let out: "I want musicians, I want drummers, and may all the poets come prepared to read, to testify in heightened language to a life lived as a lifelong sonnet." I knew I had to put the poem into action, and I knew that the whole of the community would have to help me lift the poem off the page.

That night Amiri Baraka, Pedro Pietri, Jose-Angel Figueroa, Nancy Mercado, Eddie Figueroa, Julio Dalmau, Amina Baraka, Louis Reyes Rivera, Luis Guzman, and many, many other writers, musicians, and friends showed up to celebrate the passing of a man who had left a legacy of poetry and theater behind.

When a poet dies, a whole community is affected, and the Lower East Side was abuzz with despair, sadness, and the keen awareness of the solitude that was coming. We all knew we would no longer see Miky on the streets of the Lower East Side, giving and taking at will whatever and whenever he wanted.

The preparations for the ceremony of the scattering of the ashes forged an unbreakable bond between the artists and the working people of the Lower East Side. Miky had asked that his ashes be scattered

> *From Houston to 14th Street*
> *from Second Avenue to the mighty D*

He wanted his ashes scattered where

> *the hustlers & suckers meet*
> *the faggots & freaks will all get*
> *high*
> *on the ashes that have been scattered*
> *thru the Lower East Side*

Miky wanted singing. He didn't want tears. As we prepared the empty lot next to the Nuyorican Poets Cafe, people came from everywhere to join our procession. There was simply no other place to start the procession of the scattering of the ashes than the Nuyorican Poets Cafe, which he had founded with me. A wonderful installation had been created in that garbage-strewn lot by Arturo Lindsay. He had prepared an effigy to be burnt at the site. We set it on fire. The lot was perfect—not manicured, but littered and disheveled and unpretentiously alive. We had cleared only a small circle for the installation, leaving the rest in its natural state: broken glass, strewn brick, unearthed boilers, and local garbage. Drummers surrounded the installation, and our teacher Jorge Brandon spoke the first words. Brandon, the great master of the oral tradition at the ripe young age of eighty-five, spoke with accuracy and pitch that belied his age and appearance. He stepped up, read a poem, then dropped it into the fire; as that poem burned another poet would step forward, recite, then drop a poem into the flames. It was clear that Miky's instructions had been letter-perfect. His poem continued:

> There's no other place for me to be
> there's no other place that I can see
> there's no other town around that
> brings you up or keeps you down
> no food little heat sweeps by
> fancy cars & pimps' bars & juke saloons
> & greasy spoons make my spirits fly
> with my ashes scattered thru the
> Lower East Side . . .

The poem began to leap off the page and become the thing itself—words were becoming action.

I was handed the quart-sized can that contained Miky's ashes. My hands trembled, and Joey Castro took the can from me. I asked him to please open it. He pulled out his pocketknife and began to pry the lid off gently, respectfully, and yet fearfully. I'll never forget the look on his face when the lid popped off lightly and we saw the ashes for the very first time. How very odd—the frame of a man weighs less than two and a half pounds of dust. And what did I have in the quart can? I had the ashes of a man who proclaimed himself . . .

> *A thief, a junkie I've been*
> *committed every known sin*
> *Jews and Gentiles. . . . Bums and Men*
> *of style . . . run away child*
> *police shooting wild . . .*
> *mother's futile wails . . . pushers*
> *making sales . . . dope wheelers*
> *& cocaine dealers . . . smoking pot*
> *streets are hot & feed off those who bleed to death . . .*
>
> *all that's true*
> *all that's true*
> *all that is true*
> *but this ain't no lie*
> *when I ask that my ashes be scattered thru*
> *the Lower East Side.*

So the procession left the yard on the west side of the Cafe and began its voyage through the Lower East Side in concurrence with the configuration that the poem had laid out: *From Houston to 14th Street/from Second Avenue to the mighty D.* As we walked, I would scatter the ashes and people would say, "Who's that, who goes there?" The answer would initially come from me, "It's Miky Pinero." The response would be astounding. "It's Miky Pinero!" One person would cry out, and then another, "It's Miky Pinero," and then another, "It's Miky Pinero." It was a litany, the repetition of the rosary. People passed the word out in waves of sorrow, communicating to each other that the dispersal had begun, that Miky's ashes were being spread. Pinero was having the burial of his dreams, his poem breathing, moving, and bouncing people. By the time we reached Avenue D the procession was huge. People walking their dogs, going into stores, and standing at bus stops would forget the object of their mission and join us. It was as if they were impelled by a force bigger than themselves. If they were on their way to work, they didn't go. If they were on their way to the stores, they wouldn't go. If they were going to the park, they didn't go. If they were walking their dog, they joined us. The murmuring grew into an audible incantation, "It's Miky Pinero, it's the poet, it's the guy who wrote *Short Eyes* (a well-known play and film by Miguel Pinero), it's the guy on TV, on *Miami Vice,* it's the guy that gave me twenty dollars when I needed it." It was the man that we all knew by many names and in many places.

Great ceremonies are followed by cataclysmic changes. After the procession ended, a great food-and-drink reception had been planned at Roland Legiardi-Laura's loft. The planning for the reception had been spontaneous and exciting. Roland had permitted the use of his place for the send-off of a great poet, and I had found what I was searching for: a big, well-lit space where we could all come to make an offering after the scattering of the ashes. The wake would be accompanied by great food, drink, and recitals. In the midst of this rejoicing, Bob Holman approached me and said, "Miguel, it's time to reopen the Cafe. This is the moment, you know, and Miky is insisting on it, and we are ready. Let's move on it, let's open the Nuyorican Poets Cafe again." . . . Yes, Miky's death was to be a new beginning. From the ashes, life.

The final threshhold that all of us must cross is as thin and porous as a veil. Only a breath separates the living and the dead. Yet it also is an iron door that locks behind, from which no traveler returns. In our most meaningful rituals we figuratively recreate death's threshold and traverse it with symbolic acts. In a language of symbols and ritual actions, we refuse to give death the last word.

FIVE

Commemorative Art

Human beings are made of perishable stuff; not rock or wood or precious metal, but flesh and blood. Yet our ability to create and manipulate symbols enables us to associate ourselves with the durable. Many of us leave a succinct record of our lives carved into stone, on headstones and gravestones; and we encase our bodies in wood to lie them in the earth.

We use commemorative art to immortalize our lives in objects that can outlast mortal bodies by years, sometimes centuries. This art continues to illuminate our lives to those who see it. This section looks at the way some of our contemporaries have crafted material objects to contain memory.

The process of creating art can be as important as the final product. It provides those grieving the loss of their own lives or the loss of loved ones, with a focus, a project. The act of creation satisfies. And it counters the annihilation wrought by death. Crafting commemorative art translates the physical expression of love and sorrow into a physical representation of those feelings.

A recurrent theme in commemorative art is the co-existence of public and private meanings. Intimate expressions of love and grief are openly expressed in the rather public space of the cemetery, for example, but private meanings also can be encoded into cemetery art. Those who are not privy to the symbolism in a particular piece of commemorative art appreciate it at a more abstract level than those who knew the person whose life is being commemorated. And even those who knew the deceased might not be aware of all the meanings put into the art by its maker.

The arts of music and dance are also used to physically commemorate the dead. In New Orleans, for instance, many musicians have been honored with jazz funerals. In this traditional African-American ceremony, the band meets at the funeral parlor or church and proceeds through the neighborhood where the deceased lived and worked, and then on to the cemetery. After the interment, the musicians lead the procession from the gravesite in silence. At a respectful distance from the site, the lead trumpeter sounds a two-note riff, alerting his fellow musicians, who shed solemnity and begin to improvise and play upbeat tunes. The party of family and friends begin to strut and bring out elaborately decorated umbrellas.

The infectious spirit of these New Orleans jazz funerals is mirrored in a number of personal responses to death. Guthrie Ramsey, who grew up in a musical family on Chicago's south side, recounts that when his father died, the formal funeral and staid restaurant gathering somehow did not seem adequate in memorializing his father or in dealing with the family's grief. They decided to mark the death in the same manner they had often celebrated life—with a house party. "The family met a few days later for a 'home-cooked' celebration. The food and drink were good and plentiful, and the music was just right—a little jazz, a little rhythm and blues, a little funk, a little soul." As the music, the food and drink, the conversation and laughter reached a familiar combustible pitch, the family chose partners and stepped out onto a makeshift dance floor. "As the evening progressed, the young and not so young, aunts with nephews, brothers with sisters, cousins with cousins, . . . danced, played cards, 'stomped the blues,' and stomped our grief away with the blues. Auntie Ethel would refer to such events as 'good times like the Ramseys do like,' even if the reasons for gathering were not always happy ones. And although the spoons my father would have played laid still on the table, we finished the job and partied for him."

Creating A Place For the Dead

The coffin of C. B. (Chevene Bowers) King, Esq., a prominent black Civil Rights attorney who represented Martin Luther King Jr. (no relation) among others, reflected his modesty. "It was so much him," his daughter told us. "His whole image of exiting this world was really about the elegance of simplicity—being simply buried in something that's crafted by your children."

When Peggy King-Jorde and her brother made their father's coffin, at his request, she felt she was creating a safe place that would embrace him.

Peggy's father had, in turn, created a place for his family to be together in death. Long before he died or even knew he had cancer, he had the family plot redone. One change was the addition of a King family stone inscribed with a message that he wrote addressed to those who would read the marker:

LET WHAT GOOD THERE HAS BEEN IN THE LIVES WE'VE LIVED
BE A MODEL TO LIVES YET UNSPENT AND THOSE THAT COME
AFTER.

LET OUR OCCASIONAL DEEDS OF COURAGE AND THE LOFTY
HOPES AND DREAMS WHICH MARKED OUR EARTHLY VIGIL BE
YOUR INHERITANCE TO GIRD YOU IN YOUR REACH FOR THE
UNCERTAINTIES OF FOREVER.

LET OUR PAST VISIONS OF TOMORROW'S FULFILLMENT BE FOR
YOU THIS MOMENT'S HEEDED CHALLENGE, AND

LET IT BE IN YOUR FAREWELL THAT YOU WILL HAVE KEPT
AGLOW THE FRAGILE SPARKS OF LIFE'S TRUSTS TO ILLUMINE
THE WAY AND MAKE SAFE THE LEGIONS OF HANNIBAL THAT
WILL FOLLOW.

"Basically, he wrote his own epitaph," says Peggy.

When she was working on her father's coffin, a splinter pierced her hand. She did not remove it until after the funeral was over. When she took it out, she taped it onto a page of the Bible given to her by her parents the previous Christmas during her father's illness. She placed it on the page provided for listing family deaths. She wrote, "A splinter from my hand. Leland and I built Dad's pine casket." The Bible's pages also hold a curl of her father's hair, wrapped in tissue.

The process of making of her father's coffin was much more than physical labor and craftsmanship. It was an event. Peggy's account reveals how the process took on a ceremonial richness that lured community members into it.

CRAFTING A VESSEL FOR MY FATHER
—Told by Peggy King-Jorde

My father always had a problem with coffins. He always used to say to my mother, "I want to be cremated." My mother was totally not going for that. He had a notion of his ashes being scattered in his garden so that he would always be there. He had this image of just sort of living on in the garden. My father had a client who was an undertaker, who told him that many times the ashes the family receives are really not the right ashes. So he thought, "Well, I'm not going to do that."

He had a very dear friend who was a minister who lived in southwest Georgia. When he died, this man was buried in a simple pine coffin on a hill under a tree. And my father absolutely *loved* that as an image and as a treatment of death. He used to say to all of us, my four brothers and me, "I want you to *build* me a coffin." But death, at the time, was so far away for us. So we didn't think anything of it.

When my father died, we were standing around his bed in the hospital. It was in Tijuana, Mexico, because he had cancer and he was there for alternative treatment. So we were all standing around holding hands in the hospital. And, at that moment, we were actually happy that he was dead because he had been in so much pain. He looked so restful. But then somebody said, "What's next?"

And one of my brothers said, "Well, Dad always said he wanted us, his children, to build his coffin."

And so my mother looked at my brother Leland and me because Leland had also gone to school for architecture. And she said, "Okay, you two design and build Dad's coffin."

And so after the body was flown back to Albany, Georgia, which was our home, my brother and I sat in our family room and drew sketches of the coffin on the back of an envelope for the shape, and decided on the wood and how we were going to do the handles—we wanted sisal rope handles. We designed it in a long, fairly deep rectangular shape, and we put in tongue-in-groove planks that interlocked with one another and a flat top.

The funeral home we were using was a new place. It wasn't the traditional funeral home that everybody always used to go to. The woman who was the funeral director was very supportive. We said, "We're not interested in buying a coffin; we want to build one."

She said, "Fine. I'll make one of my carpenters available. He has a truck, and he'll help you." The next morning we got up and met with the carpenter. He took us into a supply store. We collected everything we needed down to the hinges and screws and the sisal rope.

Then another friend of the family who made drapes and worked with fabric showed us an off-white, linen cloth for us to line the coffin with. And we asked her to make a small cushion to line the bottom and a small pillow.

We took the supplies to the funeral home, which was just a block or two from the house where our father was born. The funeral home was in a big old Victorian house. It had a beautiful big back porch. The house was on the corner and faced one street, but you could see the porch from the side. This is a neighborhood where people sit on their porches, like they do in the South. People would walk by on the sidewalk and stop to talk and see what was happening.

My father was very prominent, and everyone expected him to be in a very expensive coffin. So when word had it that his kids were making his coffin, people would come up on the back porch to see.

It was a beautiful Spring day. And everybody was sitting out on the banisters and there was lemonade. And on the sawhorses we had this coffin we were crafting.

It was funny—people would come up on the porch, but they wouldn't talk about the coffin. They'd simply sit, especially a lot of the elderly people. They'd sit on the edge and they'd ask how everybody was doing, and they'd almost ignore the coffin. I think in a way, they were kind of amazed that it was actually happening. And there was an elderly man who was walking along the street—it was lined with pecan trees and the branches formed a canopy above—and he stopped and looked back at us, and walked a little, and stopped, and looked back, and eventually came over to the porch.

The whole experience of being out on the porch was like a performance, particularly with this elderly man, who watched from afar and eventually decided to come up on the porch, and sit, and sort of join and watch, and not really talk about what was going on. People want to come as close as they can to certain events. Onlookers transcend and sort of transport themselves into a certain situation.

We spent time sanding the coffin down and just making sure the grain was very pretty. And our friend came over with the fabric, and he lined the inside of the coffin and put in the cushion. We started at 6 A.M., and we were finished by that afternoon.

I have such a wonderful memory of crafting the coffin. Maybe because it was such a beautiful day. What I remember was that it really was just so *satisfying*. I felt like I was creating this very safe environment for my father. I knew that he wasn't really in his shell anymore, but there was just something very *satisfying* about creating this safe place for him. And then after we completed it, our family enjoyed knowing that, "Okay, now we're ready to sort of let go."

When I was working on my father's coffin, I felt a sense of mission, of purpose. The whole process of crafting and designing it helped my brothers and me to transcend our fears associated with death—not death itself but the *effects* of death—how it impacted our family. My father had a very prominent place in the family, and everybody tended to rely on him. When I was working on the coffin, my focus was not much further beyond what was *there*, at that time and place, dealing with my brothers and other family members.

Some of my friends imagine that it would have been a morbid or sad experience, but it really wasn't. It wasn't morbid. It wasn't sad. It was just totally contrary to that. It was so *satisfying*. I would highly recommend it to anyone.

Once my father was placed inside the coffin, we put a spray of green on top. We had designed the floral spray that goes on top of the coffin, which was really not floral at all. My father really loved his garden, which was filled not so much with flowers but with various textures of green. He liked flowers, but he was not big on flower gardens. He *really* liked gardens that stayed green throughout the winter months. He would talk about the varying *shades* of green and, to him, *that* was the real beauty of his garden. So we went to a florist and picked out varying shades of green and shapes of leaves and designed a spray in all these various shades to create a texture. And we placed one red rose, which was a symbol of love, in the center.

A photo of the coffin appeared in the local newspaper and made quite a splash. Other funeral directors actually called our funeral director to find out where she got the coffin. And people were saying they wanted to be buried in the same kind of coffin that my father was buried in. They talked about how simple and yet how beautiful it was. People, I think, were moved by the fact that the *family made* the coffin, particularly that the children had made it. My aunt turned to me and said, "You guys have to do my coffin, too." My aunt was saying this as tears were flowing down her face. "I want the same thing for me. You guys have to build a coffin for me."

At the funeral people repeatedly said, "I want my children to do that," or, "I would love for you guys to do that for me." I think what appealed to people was the love that was put into it, and the sincerity that was put into it.

Somehow crafting this special place, this special vessel, was beautiful to a lot of people. I think it appealed to them in its simplicity. Many of them thought that because my father was so prominent he would be sent off in a *golden* coffin with *tons* of flowers. People were caught off guard because the emphasis was not about that, it was about something else. The richness came not out of the purchasing of materials but out of the experience of crafting the coffin and taking care of our own. I think it caused people get in touch with what this was all about. It conveyed the idea that this home-made coffin was "a safe place."

My father wanted his coffin to be very simple, and he didn't want a lot of money spent sending him off. Some people, like my father and me, hold these very morbid ideas about store-bought coffins lined with all kinds of stuff and fluff. It's gaudy. He had all kinds of design issues with that. And then the whole notion of a metal coffin was even more morbid. It was like, "What do you expect to preserve? Do you expect to go and open this coffin up later on down the line? Why would you have a metal coffin?" He liked the notion that in a simple pine coffin that would deteriorate, he was going back to the earth—the notion that death is a part of life, and that it's part of this larger circle.

Part of the ceremony at the graveside is that they lower the coffin a little just as kind of a gesture and then everybody leaves. Then the gravediggers do the real burial. But as the coffin is being lowered, I'm sitting next to my brother Leland and we realize that the coffin lid, which was designed with a little lip around the perimeter, is just a touch too big—so that if they lowered the coffin too much it was going to start lifting off. We didn't necessarily want the coffin nailed or screwed shut. We just figured it's going to go into the ground and deteriorate and that's it. And they start lowering it, and the lid is close to lifting off. And we're looking at it, my brother and I, and we're sitting there trying to give an eye to the guy who's operating this thing to tell him, "Okay you can't lower it anymore." So there was a level of comedy. And word has it from the funeral director that after everyone left they actually had to get a saw to trim off a quarter of an inch from the lid so that they could lower the coffin. We thought it was really funny. We thought, "Okay . . . alright . . . some design flaws." My father would have thought it was funny.

But still, at the burial I felt an enormous level of pride because there were so many compliments on the coffin. People kept coming up and saying, "My *God* the coffin is so *gorgeous*." It was a very simple coffin, but I think that what people were seeing was the result of this collaboration among the children. A part of me went into the coffin. It's like any artist who feels there's part of them in something they've created. I felt that my brother Leland and I represented all my brothers in making the coffin. It's a part of all of us. It was something that *we* crafted and *we* created and so it was this sort of personal embrace that was going to be with my father's shell always. Creating the vessel gave us a sense of comfort. I felt that there was a part of each of us put into the coffin. That's what made it good, and that's what made it a safe place.

Art at the End of Life

Jane Cameron is an artist and photographer from Hastings-on-Hudson, New York. When her children reached school age, Jane went back to get a degree in photography at the International Center for Photography. While she was in school, her mother died suddenly. In the months that followed her mother's death, Jane found herself assembling and photographing bark, fallen leaves, seed pods, and soil from places that were dear to her and her mother. "These things spoke a language of grief that I couldn't put into words," she said.

Jane's own grieving process led her to volunteer for the hospice movement. After years of working closely with the dying, she shifted her attention from those who were dying to those managing the effects of death on their lives. She is now the Director of School Outreach at The Bereavement Center of Westchester in Tuckahoe, New York.

Early on, Jane's photography and her work with hospice began to merge. She realized that art could help people as they died. When her friend Rose, a fellow artist in the village of Hastings-on-Hudson, was diagnosed with cancer, Jane drew on her photography to co-create a project that encouraged Rose to review what she considered best about her life as she was coping with life-threatening illness. Focusing on what she calls 'the power of pillows,' Jane took the ideas she developed with Rose into her work with the dying and the bereaved. Her work with pillows encourages both dying and grieving individuals to physically embrace their cherished memories.

"I'VE BEEN A GOOD LIFE"
—Told by Jane Cameron

Rose Reitter was a friend of mine from Hastings who died in 1993. She lived in town and she was a potter, a musician, and a poet. I met her through the arts council years ago. She taught my sons pottery when one was in the third grade and two were in the fifth grade. We spent a whole winter meeting every three or four weeks. She helped us make beautiful things together—that's how I came to know her and love her as a teacher and a potter. I also knew her as a singer with the Hudson Valley Singers who came to our home and serenaded us with Christmas carols. She made me a beautiful piece of pottery. It was the most wonderful gift.

Rose was in her mid-fifties when she contracted abdominal cancer. So what I did—as an artist speaking to an artist—was ask her if she'd be interested in finding an art form through which we could help her come to terms with her illness and celebrate her life.

Together we believed that if we could find the images that captured her most fundamental sources of power, they would help her in her quest to heal the woundedness in her life, and perhaps even find a cure. In the beginning we didn't talk about dying, we talked about healing. The first efforts were to find a healer. I introduced her to a woman who did hands-on healing. My friend did a session with her, and I photographed this woman's hands on Rose. I developed the pictures, and I asked Rose to meditate on these photographs. My thought was that she would have the actual experiences with the healer, and after that, she could use the photographs to call back that healing with her eyes and her imagination. She said it made her feel better, but it didn't save her.

I have a strong belief, especially when you're in the end-stage of life, that it's not about curing but about healing. Healing is about reconciling yourself to relationships—inward or interpersonal or spiritual—that need clarity and closure. The art was a way for me to connect with her. I couldn't say, "How is the cancer progressing?" But I could say, "How are you using the images? When are you using them?" The art process was a wonderful sieve through which we communicated with each other. I could ask her, subtly, "How are you really doing?" and she had the opening to say what she needed to say about how she was using the artwork and how she was feeling.

As Rose grew sicker and sicker, I moved to this idea of the pillow. It came very organically with the demise of her physicalness—she couldn't hold a print and sit in front of it and meditate. It became obvious that an exterior image of someone laying hands on her was no longer effective because they were somebody else's hands.

So I said, "What images give you energy?" She took me through her photographic images of herself. We looked through her pictures of her years as a young mother, and I asked her, "Which of these images remind you of your power?" We spent hours talking about her life and which images reminded her of her innate power—not just the images she liked, but those that reminded her of herself.

For me, the powerful images are those that depict you when you felt yourself to be truly who you were—out there in the world, totally *there* in the world. They were images of her that reminded her of herself as a powerful human being. Those were the pictures of her as an incredibly loving mother and as a very creative, funky artist. Those were the two places, the two valences where she invited me via photographs into her life. And then they started to jibe, and in the alchemy of those two valences she would sit and look at those photographs and say, "I've had a good life. I've been a good life."

I took slides of those photographs, and I started to think about finding a place where she could comfortably access them. For me, images on a wall seem to be at a secondary distance. So these two ideas came together simultaneously—one was using her images; the other was creating something that she could touch, hold, and literally be with. That's where I came up with the idea of putting the images on pillows.

I actually believe in the totemic power of both the cloth and the image. If you can develop pillow images from your own life story and then lie on them, there's a vibrational magic. You're creating your own shroud in a way, a shroud to use for living.

So I made Rose a collage pillow, and she loved it. That was the first of many pillows that I made both with people who were dying and with those who were grieving. I made a photographic pillow for one woman whose family was so touched by the way she used it as she was dying that they placed the pillow in the casket with her. Then, at the bereavement center where I work now, I introduced the pillow project. Every child who goes through our program makes a pillow in honor of and in memory of their parent who died. Some kids make them so they can hug them, and others put their pillow on their bed or near their bed as a way of remembering. The children tell us, years later, that the close presence and feel of the pillow in the space before sleep gives them a sense of comfort with their own grief and an ongoing connection to the person they lost.

Legacies

At the Veterans Hospital in St. Albans, Queens, an artist named C Bangs worked with frail and elderly patients to create collages about their lives. Sponsored by Elders Share the Arts, an organization in New York City, the project was called Legacy Works. The first week of the project, C Bangs met with the patients, each one facing imminent death, and talked with them about their lives. She brought in magazines so they could select images that captured their experience; she also looked through their family photos with them. "This would be their legacy," she said, "their statement about themselves."

In the next week of the project she drew their portraits in pencil and charcoal. Then, together they created the collages to surround the portraits. One man, for instance, was interested in theater, and he selected images of people in theatrical poses. "He was interested in ladies, so we had a lady or two."

In her conversations with one man, C Bangs discerned his sense of guilt for the way he had lived his life. In the process of selecting images for the collage, they came across a series of angels that they cut out and included in his portrait. "As I put the angels around his head, he said, 'Well, if I look like that I must not be going to hell—I must be going to heaven.' Suddenly, it seemed to me like he felt better about his life."

C Bangs completed twenty-four of these collages in the hospital. Every one of the portraits was framed as part of the project and either given to the families or hung on the walls of the ward. "In a ward of the frail and elderly," she continued, "where the focus is on caring for all the millions of details around a body, it seems that's what people became. So this collaborative portrait was their way of saying, 'No, I am not just a body. This is who I am.' "

C Bangs (her name shortened from Constance), also used her artistic talent to cope with her father's dying. She recalls her father as "a very striking man, a very striking figure."

DRAWING FATHER
—Told by C Bangs

Around the same time that I was working at the VA hospital in 1994, I went back home to take care of my father. He had been ill for years, and he had been steadily declining. Initially he could get up and sit in a chair, and then he was confined to a wheelchair, and finally he was completely bedridden.

When it looked like he was getting close to dying, I went home and stayed with him and my mother. By that point he wasn't even able to talk because of a cancer in his throat, and so I would simply sit at his bedside with him. I would just sit and talk to him. Then finally, I remembered that I'm an artist, and I thought I'd like to draw him.

My father seemed to feel good about it. It was an easy social interaction. I was just drawing to be with him. Sometimes a neighborhood child would come in. I remember a young girl named Zoe who was like a granddaughter to him would sit with me and draw on top of my drawing.

My father was an engineer and he first taught me how to draw. Like any kid, I drew a lot. My grandfather had sent me a picture of a horse pulling a sled. One day when I was six years old I told my father I would really like to be able to draw like that. So we had a lesson and subsequent lessons.

The act of drawing him was very much a part of who I am and of our interaction. Our relationship had been very close, and drawing was a way to be with him in the way that expresses who I am. It wasn't an easy relationship, but it was a close relationship.

The day he died, I had been drawing, and drawing, and drawing all morning. Then the hospice nurse came in to relieve us so that we could have some lunch. As we were going out, I took out my camera and photographed him with my mother. I now treasure those beautiful images of the two of them holding hands. We went out and had lunch, and when we returned, my mother went to lie down for a few minutes. When I went into my father's room, I could see he was in the process of dying. And so I called in my mother and we were with him when he died.

He went the way he wanted to go—at home, peacefully. And we had time to sit with the body, which was actually very healing and grounding. I photographed him then, too.

I put together the program for my father's memorial service. My father was very interested in metaphysics. I took one of the last drawings I did of him when he was dying down to a Xerox place, and I had them superimpose one of my father's philosophical writings on to it. On the program for his memorial service, his face, as I had drawn it in his final days, shone through his words: "As time passes through and/or around us, we will always be in the now, whether in this life or the next. In truth, there is only now . . . the eternal now. We are eternally conscious of the here and now."

A Weekly Memorial

Every Sunday for the past eight years, rain or shine, with no vacations, a jazz concert takes place in the parlor of Marjorie Eliot's home on what she calls the northern tip of Harlem. Marjorie, who comes from a long line of musicians, lives in a landmarked building on Edgecombe Avenue where Duke Ellington and Paul Robeson once lived. In 1992, one of Marjorie's five children, her son Philip, also a musician, passed away at the age of thirty-one. Her way of celebrating her son is through a series of weekly concerts in her living room. The landlord loves the concerts, and they are open to anyone with a few hours to spare on Sunday afternoons. Cookies and orange juice are served to the guests.

MUSIC TO REMEMBER HIM
—Told by Marjorie Eliot

I always knew how to play music. When I was growing up in Philadelphia, it seemed to me that everybody did. We had two pianos in my house—I don't know why. My great-grandmother played. We all played. Maybe the part of Africa that we're from was where the artists and musicians came from. I don't know what else to attribute it to. I had to practice the piano before doing my other homework because it was all one piece—it was part of my homework. I brought up my children the same way. I grew up with this music—what I call African-American classical music—jazz. It was always there.

When my son Philip was thirty, he took sick. He was on dialysis, and we had a lot of time on our hands. I did all the nursing tasks. I really took care of him. It was the least I could do. It kind of forgives you for not being a perfect parent. I would play music for him in the parlor just to make the day happy. He would sit in his wheelchair, and I would read plays or play music for him.

The Sunday that he died, I came home and I played the piano for hours and hours. I played a lot of songs he'd heard, and I played some new songs that he had never heard out of the Oscar Peterson book. It helped me. I was in shock, and I stopped screaming enough to concentrate on the piano, so it was healing.

I was in terrible shape after he died. I can remember I went to Jewish Family Services the day after the memorial. I spoke to this really lovely, sensitive man named Rappaport. I said, "Well, I really came because everybody said I should come talk about this." When I said that I started crying.

Then he said, "You're doing good. We're not supposed to bury our children." He had a picture of his children on his desk.

He asked me how I was feeling, and I said, "Well, I have a teddy bear of Phillie's that I'm sleeping with."

He said, "Anything you need to do."

He held my hand, and we just talked. And he said, "You don't need me." He had a great smile.

But Phil died on a Sunday, and every Sunday I would scream—understandably. I would have my little nervous breakdown every Sunday leading up to his birthday, July 18th. I can remember thinking, "I'm not getting through this."

But I kept remembering how he always said, "Mommy, I don't want you to let this knock you out"—we never used the word "death"—"I want you to act and sing and play the piano and do all those things." So this was something that he handled very well.

I desperately wanted to find a way to celebrate him. Finally, a year of Sundays passed by, and I had to prepare for the Sunday that would mark the one-year anniversary of his death. I wondered, "How am I going to celebrate that anniversary?"

Then I had the idea of playing music in his honor. He loved music, and I had played for him when he was sick. Now I would play in order to remember him.

And then I started thinking about all the musicians I've known for many years, like Bob Cunningham, one of the premiere bassists in the world. So I called and said that I wanted to do a concert in honor of Phil. He said, "Great, all right. What time?" My husband, Al Drears, is a drummer who has played with everyone in the world, so I knew these extraordinarily gifted people. It wasn't anything to get them—I had to worry about the audience.

Once I did it at the anniversary, I decided to do it every Sunday. I can remember asking my neighbor Rachel Kent the first time I was going to do it, "Rach, do you think I can get any people?"

"Of course!"

"Do you think it's a good idea?"

"Of course!"

And it's true. She comes every Sunday and sits right there. She loves the music. I get some serious listeners, some very serious listeners.

I still cry. And why not? But I know that I got this right, celebrating him in this quiet way. I'm trying to be worthy of his love for me—because he was crazy about me. So I'm really working on being deserving of his love. I don't see it as sacrificing to do it; I see it as my life depends on it. I have to do it.

Mourning Quilts

In Victorian times, mourning quilts were often pieced out of the clothing of the departed. The women who made them were helped, as they sewed, to physically work through their grief. The tradition has been revived by contemporary women, including a Boston fabric artist named Kathleen Doyle, who creates mourning quilts for clients who commission her to help them commemorate the lives of their loved ones.

Commissioning commemorative art is, in itself, a creative response to death. As Sheryl Mullane-Corvi, a client who worked with Kathleen to design a quilt, described it, "Because you did let me collaborate and make suggestions, I felt that it expressed what I wanted to express—with you doing the artwork."

Kathleen has great appreciation for the history of particular fabrics and great sensitivity to the memories and emotions associated with them. "I use fabric from old clothing or dish towels—fabric from their lives," says Kathleen. "At funeral parlors today, grieving is so homogenized. It's kind of become a generic process—something people want to get over with. There's hardly any individuality at many ceremonies, and mourners are left cold and unsatisfied. At least that's what I've seen. I had an awful feeling after going to so many funerals of people I've known. There never seemed to be a trace of the person's vitality or of the unique happiness in the person's life in the ceremonies. The quilts *celebrate* the person's individual life."

This attitude has also led her to create coffin quilts to cover caskets during funerals. "They drape coffins in a cozy, warm embrace," she says. "The family of the deceased design it to mourn and honor the life of the deceased and then it is left with the family as a remembrance."

Quilts are intimately connected to the cycle of life, in Kathleen's view. "We make love on or under quilts. We enjoy deep slumber wrapped in quilts. We spend sleepless nights with quilts when we're sick. We wrap babies in quilts. They are all about sex, living, and dying."

Kathleen is generally contacted to make mourning quilts about a year after someone has died. "I find sometimes after a person dies, people don't want to go to that person's room right away and clean it out and empty out the drawers and go through all the papers. Some people like to leave it, just let it be. But when they start to clean it up, they have all these possessions and they're not sure what to do with them—maybe give them to charity or maybe give them to relatives. Usually after the dust clears from that cleaning, that's when they'll come to me."

Through Kathleen's quilts, fabric that was part of the life of the departed gets incorporated into the life of their family. "People seem to bring really specific ideas to me—how they want to wrap themselves up, like a hug, in a way that they can't do with an old pair of jeans. But if I put the pocket from the jeans into a quilt, they can actually wrap themselves in the person's jeans . . . The family has the quilt and takes it home and can use it on their bed and to physically warm themselves. I want to mirror some kind of transcendence. The clothing is no longer useful. I can cut it up and give it a new life and a new function that no one imagined during its life."

Because fabrics can evoke memories, a mourning quilt can be overwhelmingly powerful. Kathleen recounts that one family did not want their quilt right away, and that some families get emotional and want to be alone with their quilts.

Kathleen's client Sheryl Mullane-Corvi commissioned her to make a memorial to her father, Thomas Mullane. "The only tangible thing she had left of him was an old shirt, a beige, plaid shirt, an old favorite that he used to wear a lot. I cut the shirt up along with other fabrics representative of his life and made a quilt as an artwork for the wall."

Sheryl is particularly dedicated to keeping her father's memory alive. He was the only boy in a family of three, and both his children were girls. "So the Mullanes are dead. He was the end of the line. That's why I kept my name." She designed a headstone for her father bearing a Celtic cross, but it didn't come out as she had envisioned. "I was looking for a suitable memorial, and it didn't do it for me."

The two-by-three-foot quilt hangs in Sheryl's living room in Melrose, Massachusetts. It is comprised of four blocks, each a different color, each containing parts of the beige plaid shirt, and each with a splash of red in the center. Kathleen describes the design as "a kind of hacked up, funky version of a very traditional pattern called the log cabin."

So many years passed between the time Sheryl's father died and the time she commissioned the quilt that "the grieving was done," as she put it, and she could celebrate his life. For Sheryl, it seems, the quilt evokes her father's essence, just as a good eulogy can bring the essence of the person being remembered into the room.

PORTRAIT OF A PERSONALITY
—Told by Sheryl Mullane-Corvi

Each block of the quilt has part of my father's shirt in it. And each color in the quilt represents a facet of my father's personality. The first block on the left is the purple, because he could be quirky and silly. He'd be in the kitchen, and my mother would be cooking and trying to brush him away, and he'd just grab her and they'd polka. My mother would push him away and finish making supper. He could be like that.

The green was for his Irish ancestry. The browns were because he was a carpenter and a woodworker. And the blue was for the calm and steadfast family man, which is what he was. Then you have some brown, blue, purple, and green, representing the different facets, which he balanced really well, all around the border. We talked about putting parts of his shirt in the border, too, but we decided that the shirt should concentrate in the four personality blocks.

I was also envisioning red because he had an Irish temper. He could be happy and cheerful and then, at the drop of a hat—you screw up and boy you wanted to run like hell. But you didn't see that very much. It was just really quick flashes of anger. So red wasn't supposed to be dominant. It was Kathleen's idea to fix the red in the center of each block to represent the hearth, because he was centered in the home. She told me that in traditional log cabin quilts, red, representing the hearth, is in the center of each block.

My friend Kelly's mother met my father. I thought she described him really well as "a generous man with a twinkle in his eye." I was thinking of that when I was trying to incorporate things into the quilt. I didn't know how you would signify that, but I think it's there. My intention was that the quilt would be a portrait of his personality. And when I see it, I remember what he was like.

The Shirt

The shirt was what he was wearing the last time I saw him. I didn't set out to get it. I just took it because my mother's the type of person who doesn't like clutter. So on one of my trips up to visit her in New Hampshire after he died, I remember thinking she was starting to throw things away and that I should take it. I just grabbed it.

I took the shirt which *happened* to be really typical of him because it was plaid and it was beige and he always wore plaid. Unfortunately, his theory was that plaid goes with plaid, so he would wear plaid plants and a plaid shirt. Stripes go with stripes. Polka dots go with polka dots. And everything was shades of brown.

I had this shirt, it was just hanging around. For a while, it was on a big teddy bear I had so I wouldn't lose it. But then I went through ten apartments in five years and it kept just getting stuffed into different places. It was on that bear for I don't know how long. My father died in '91 and I just had the quilt made now, in '99. So this shirt was traipsing around for eight years before I did anything with it. The teddy bear was stuffed in the closet. It wasn't a case of wanting to look at the shirt or anything, it was just a case of making sure I had it.

I don't know how to quilt, but I always knew that eventually I would figure out how to do it and I would make a quilt or do something with the shirt. I didn't realize that this kind of quilt had been made before. I thought I was being really original. I didn't realize there was a Victorian tradition. All I knew was I had this wad of material that I was lugging around.

If I had done this eight years ago, one year after he died, what I wanted wouldn't have been the same. I think I wouldn't have had anything specific in mind. It would have just been, "Do whatever you want with this shirt," because everything was still chaotic and I hadn't worked through emotions or come to terms with things. I think the chaos would have been part of what the quilt would have looked like.

Nine years passed and I was able to form these opinions of my father as a man so that the outcome is different now. Nine years ago I don't think I knew him as well. He was still "Dad." And now, nine years later, he's an individual.

SACRED FABRIC
—Told by Kathleen Doyle

When I first received the shirt I asked myself, "What is this? Who am I to this?"

Some of the fabrics I use in my work are bought new, some I get in vintage stores, and some are my own grandmother's old fabrics from her sewing basket or even her clothing. So there's this whole personal collage of fabrics for me to use. And then someone in Sheryl's position gives me a new fabric—a total curve ball, a total foreigner coming into my world. I don't really have the emotional history with this new fabric, but it may be the most important textile. I have this kind of sacred fabric to mix in with all my other fabrics. So the more I'm with this shirt—I don't want to sound strange here, but—the more it feels like a prayer.

And I feel like I have to live up to this faith. I have to live up to what Sheryl has invested in it. I feel entrusted with something heavy. This is the shirt that her father might have had for decades and then she had for nine years. And when I make those first cuts in the fabric, I just hack away at this shirt using this big rotary cutter I have. It's really violent. I can't put it back together once it's cut. That's why I get a deposit and I have people sign and initial things, because, as I tell them, "We have to be very clear that there's no turning back."

I asked Sheryl if she wanted the little bits of the shirt that were left over—the buttons and the collar stays. I saved them in a medical examiner's way in this little plastic bag, taking the threads off the button with tweezers. I just don't feel right, 'til the whole process is done, to do anything else with them. So I have my own little rituals of what to do with the scraps.

When I cut up clothing to make a quilt, the rending of fabric is permanent. It's the end of one life and the beginning of something new. It's not a utilitarian thing anymore. It's not functional. It's not as it was intended. It's just accepting a whole new thing. I like to think this quilt brought a piece of clothing that in a way wasn't utilitarian—that was on a teddy bear in a closet that was in a kind of gray period, in transition from being worn by her father—to now. It has a new life. It has a new identity. This reflects the cycles of physical death and spiritual birth. I really like that idea of recycling, reinventing, and facilitating change. I'm making "change" touchable, giving it a welcoming texture.

The quilt is transformed—becomes a completely different object—when the viewer learns the significance of its design and the memories and associations contained within it. The quilt, like many examples of commemorative art, though publicly displayed, contains private meanings. Sheryl and Kathleen discussed how the quilt could "mean."

"It's interesting," mused Sheryl, "that although the quilt is exactly what I wanted, my father wouldn't have understood it at all."

"That fascinates me," replied Kathleen, "because when I was working with the shirt I thought about its history and how it could become an heirloom, not as a garment but as part of a quilt. But I also wondered, "Would the person who wore this have any idea what it might mean some day, or would he say, " 'Why'd you do *that*?' "

"Exactly. He'd say, 'Who'd want my old shirt?' " confirmed Sheryl.

"Based on the little morsel that I knew about your father," Kathleen continued, "as I was making the quilt I was thinking, 'Wow, if this man was here he'd probably be like, " 'Oh sweetheart, that's really nice. Isn't that lovely? But I don't really think my daughter should be wasting her time on this.' "

"I wouldn't be able to tell him I spent money on it; I would have to tell him a friend did it," Sheryl joked. "He'd say, 'Oh that's very nice. Did you have to put money into that?' "

Sheryl went on to discuss the actual reactions of her other family members. "My mother thought it was a nice thing to do, but she doesn't 'get it.' My sister asked, 'What's it supposed to be?' "

"It's not supposed to be anything. Everything doesn't have to *be* something. If it was somebody I knew would understand, I would be so excited to explain it. But if they're not going to understand, then I don't want to expose myself."

"I love that you say that," responded Kathleen, "because I'm teaching people how to make their own family quilts as living portraits, and I tell them, 'This can be your private code. This can be something that just may be beautiful to look at when a visitor comes to your house. You don't have to share what it means to you.' "

"I think the quilt was more for myself than it was for my father," concludes Sheryl. "Because I think that if it was for him, then I would explain it to everybody. The fact that I'm not doing that is indicative that it's actually for me. It's also for my son, who's named after my father. His first name is Thomas, and Mullane is his middle name. And, unfortunately, he's not going to know his grandfather. So if he ever gets to the point where he would appreciate knowing, I'd want him to know about his grandfather's personality. And the quilt will be a good place to start."

A Communal Casket Cover

Fabric lends itself to commemorative art. It has many metaphoric meanings. We speak, for example, of the "fabric of our lives" and of the ways in which lives get "woven" together. At a New York synagogue, white and ivory silk ribbons inscribed with names of the dead, and sometimes with messages to them, are woven together to create a communal casket cover and communal memory. This remembrance project was initiated by Sarah Jacobs in 1999 at Ansche Chesed on the Upper West Side of Manhattan. When finished, it will be used at congregants' funerals.

As Sarah explained in the synagogue Bulletin: "At the funeral ceremony the casket is usually covered by a decorative cloth called a *mihseh*—literally a cover or blanket. The Ansche Chesed community has been working to create a *mihseh* that is both deeply meaningful and that will cover our dead with the collective memories of our loved ones. The project will reflect and also concretely represent what we do for each other in times of mourning—times of need, and vulnerability."

"Members of the congregation purchase strips of ribbon on which they write the names of the people they want to remember. All of the individual ribbons will be woven together, as indeed our lives and memories have been woven together. The finished weaving will be used as a *mihseh,* a casket cover, at Ansche Chesed funerals. So even in death we are covered by the memories of the people who are part of our community life."

The project is subsidized by congregant Sam Schiff in appreciation of the community support he received when his mother died. The sponsorship is particularly appropriate, as she was a seamstress. The *mihseh* also functions as a fundraising project, at $54 a strip. This fits into the Jewish tradition of honoring people's memories with charitable contributions (donations to most causes are made in multiples of eighteen, which is the numerological equivalent of the Hebrew word for "life"). Ultimately the *mihseh* will be comprised of two hundred forty ribbons and will measure 5×10 feet. When the weaving is complete, Sarah will organize a communal quilting to finish it. She holds periodic weaving sessions at which people can connect their strips to others and also connect with other community members as they share the stories represented by the ribbons.

"What happens here is that the stories get woven together.

Because the people who come sort of get woven together, too," says Sarah. Indeed, the weaving sessions, which include the creation of art and ritual, are also storytelling sessions. Two women, Doris Ullendorff and Andrea Funer, participated one Sunday night. As we sat around a table, they used gold and silver pens to design memorial ribbons. They inscribed the names of those they wished to memorialize, the dates of death and birth, and drew decorative borders. While we sat, Doris told the stories behind her ribbon, memorializing her son and her paternal grandparents; Sarah Jacobs told both poignant and funny stories about her relationships with some of her husband's relatives who had died.

Because the ribbon strips are woven together, some of the writing can be read and some is concealed from the public eye. Although the people who design each ribbon know its entire text, the public only sees part of it. "This represents the public and private aspect of people's lives," explains Sarah.

Once the ribbons were complete, we moved away from the table over to chairs in another part of the room. Pinned onto an easel were ribbons that had been woven together in previous sessions. Sarah led us in a *niggun* (a melody without words), one she chose because it seems both sad and triumphant to her. Sarah asked each woman to either read the names of, or speak about, the people on her ribbon and then weave it into the *mihseh*. Then she chanted the traditional memorial prayer, "El Maleh Rachamim." The transformative power of ritual was almost tangibly present in the room.

As Andrea experienced it: "I had this unexpected feeling when I was weaving. It didn't feel mundane. It just reminded me of all these movies like *Braveheart* that have scenes where there's this culture and people respond to tragedy with very simple and concrete rituals. I never felt I had that. But the weaving is concrete and is at a whole other level. Something like that is very comforting, very satisfying."

Weaving lends itself nicely to imagery involving stories and community. The *mihseh* is comprised of individual strips, each different yet united, providing "a sense of communal loss and comfort," according to one participant. Others express that each ribbon and story is, "part of a bigger thing;" that the "people woven in can't be forgotten;" that the wovenness conveys "the idea of community meeting . . . the idea that people's lives, whether you know them or not, are intertwined."

Creativity need not always be virtuosic to be functional. Visually, the *mihseh* is not particularly stunning. Yet its potency is undeniable. Sarah commented that when you first see the *mihseh* you think, "So it's a bunch of names." But you hear the stories that go with some of the ribbons, and you realize that, "Everyone's ribbon and everyone's story is as important and as powerful. To experience this fabric at a funeral is going to create an unbelievable feeling."

Memorial Walls

In many neighborhoods of New York City, memorial murals, painted by graffiti artists on city walls, are a too-familiar part of the urban landscape. Often memorializing those who died young, sometimes violently, on the city's streets, these vibrant splashes of color amidst the gray of the city celebrate the lives of those who used to liven the streets with their presence. The memorials keep the dead in the community, in the places where they lived. They also are constant reminders of community loss, particularly the loss of young people.

Memorial walls generally include portraits of the deceased, their nicknames, dates of birth and death, and images that attempt to convey who they were and what was important to them. Family and friends help determine the design of the walls by answering the artists' questions about the person's likes, dislikes, and what they would want to be remembered for. The walls are usually painted in the community where the deceased lived or hung out.

In the 1980s, particularly in the Bronx, Harlem, and the Lower East Side, young graffiti artists began creating murals on public spaces such as handball courts and empty brick walls on the sides of stores, in memory of friends who had died. These memorial walls were appreciated by their local communities, and the artists were soon being approached to paint walls for people they did not know. Although the walls are painted in public spaces, they have personal meanings for the people who knew the deceased.

Hector "Nicer" Nazario, a founding member of the graffiti crew Tats Cru, spoke about memorial walls in his mural company's headquarters in the South Bronx. He and his friends used to paint graffiti on subway trains and now run a business painting murals of all kinds, including memorial walls and promotional advertisements. There is a memorial wall to the left of the entrance to the building. It commemorates "Mink," a young man who lived on the block before his death from cancer. "We used to hang out with his brothers," Nicer says as he shows the photo of this mural in the crew's portfolio.

Each wall has a story, and as Nicer reviews the portfolio with us, we realize that, collectively, the walls not only are a litany of causes of death but also a community history. Nicer tells of a little girl named

Iris killed by a stray bullet; young men who died of stabbings, shoot-
ings, AIDS, an asthma attack, a motorcycle accident, a car accident,
leukemia, cancer, a fire, a fall from scaffolding, and police brutality;
and elderly men who died of gangrene and heart attacks. The walls
are very much "of the community." Community artists commemorate community members, in the idiom of the community—spray
can art. And when painted, the walls become sites of community
gathering.

Memorial walls recall earlier forms of public commemoration of
the dead. Nicer remembers that when he was growing up in the
South Bronx, "If there was a death in one of the apartments, the family would put a wreath over the doorway of the apartment building.
So if you walked by the building and saw flowers over the doorway,
you knew that someone had passed away within the building. And
that was a remnant of what was going on in Puerto Rico, where, if
there was a death in the family in a certain home, they would put
flowers on the outside of the doorway so that the neighbors would
know there was a death and come over. Also, in the Bronx, if someone
was killed or died in front of a store or on a certain street, people
would make these makeshift memorial stands where they would light
candles. It was temporary, but it marked a person's passing. I guess
that tradition carried over when we started doing the memorial walls."

The tradition of marking the very place where a person died with
flowers, candles, or a cross can be seen with increasing frequency in
America—especially on sites where people have been killed in high-
way accidents. Such memorials, along with memorial walls, are
"updated versions of the simple roadside crosses often erected at the
site of an automobile accident in predominantly Catholic countries,"
according to folklorist Joseph Sciorra. Such crosses, he writes, "man-

ifest the belief that the souls of those who die unexpectedly and fail to receive the Last Rites of the Catholic Church are suffering in Purgatory . . . The marker serves, then, as a lasting reminder for passersby to pray for the person's soul and thus speed its eventual arrival into heaven."

"COMMON, EVERYDAY PEOPLE WHO WERE LOVED"
—Told by Hector Nicer-Nazario

Back in the 1980s, when we were doing our own personal graffiti on the subways and on illegal walls, we would just take a little section of a wall and write the name of a friend of ours who had passed away. We would put "RIP Tony" or something. That was our way of saying, "In memory of . . ."

But people started noticing. One of the first memorial walls *we* ever painted was in 1988 or '89. Me and my friend Bio were writing our names on these handball courts. And we had this big large space on the wall that was empty, because, the way we measured everything out, we fell short. We had this big empty space, and we didn't know what to fill it with. And somebody who lived in the projects came over to Bio and told him that his brother had just passed away. And his brother's name was Pollo, which in Spanish could mean "chicken" or "good-looking guy." So he asked Bio if he could put "Rest in Peace Pollo." I had the idea to do it like a tattoo, in the shape of a heart with a ribbon in front of it and "Rest in Peace" would be on the ribbon. So it was that simple design we did for our first memorial, which was larger than just writing it in the corner of a subway train or of a wall.

And from then on people would come over to us and ask us, "Could you do a memorial wall for us?" It started simple enough—it was just friends of ours who would ask us to do these memorial walls. So we were doing them for free. But then it turned into something where we were being asked by people who we didn't know to do memorial walls for people we didn't know. After a while we couldn't continue doing it without getting paid. So that's when it started becoming a business.

One time we were really shocked because we didn't realize how popular these memorial walls had become in certain communities here in the Bronx, in Brooklyn, and in Queens. We had gotten a call from someone we knew; his father passed away and he wanted us to paint a memorial wall.

So we go over there and we speak to the guy. And he looks like he's been crying, sort of distraught and sad. So we ask him for the basic information we need. "Do you have permission to paint at the location? Can you give us the date of birth and date of decease? What was his full name? What was his nickname? What's the best picture you have of him? How do you want to remember him? What were his likes?" Each wall gets personalized according to who the person was. So we were going through our normal checklist of what we would normally ask of family and loved ones. And we get to the part where we ask the day he was born and the day he died. Bio's getting all the information; he's writing it down. So the guy gives us the date he was born and the date he died. And Bio looks up at him and says, "That's today."

The guy says, "Yeah, he passed away this morning." So we look at him, and we're like, "Do you want to wait?"

He says, "Nah. I've made the arrangements with the funeral

home. I did what I had to do. I set everything up, and now I want the wall done."

And you know, it was scary to us because we walked out of there and me and Bio had this eerie feeling that the guy's checklist of things to do after his father had passed away was, "Get the tombstone, get the funeral home, and get Tats Cru to paint a memorial wall." Suddenly we felt like, "Oh, I don't want to be in a business like that."

We did so many memorial walls at one time that we would drive through neighborhoods and people would ask us, "Why are you here? Nobody died." It scared a lot of people in the '90s when there were so many popping up. We weren't the only ones doing them. There were a lot of teenage deaths—whether it was drug overdoses, or drug-related deaths, or just suicides. So memorial walls became a constant reminder that American youth are dying.

But the biggest misconception about these memorial walls, because of the media, was that they were all for drug dealers and bad guys. It wasn't like that. We've painted so many memorial walls, but they're not all for teenagers, and the causes of death aren't all violent or drug-related. These are average, everyday people. And the best part of these memorial walls is you didn't have to be a star, you didn't have to be a singer or famous artist. These are common, everyday people, who lived in your neighborhood, who were loved.

The art form, the form of expression of the age group and the culture that hire us to paint these memorial walls in a lot of these neighborhoods is graffiti art, spray can art. People who grew up in these neighborhoods identify with this art form. A lot of these people ask you to paint these memorial walls because you're able to relate to the struggles, the hardships out there, the adaptations you have to make in order to survive—like after someone has passed how you have to deal with it and move on, what positive things you can take from it.

STILL PART OF THE CREW

The walls are generally in the communities where these people lived. It's their way of having their friends still within the community—still being part of the crew, still being part of all the guys, the gang. Memorial walls became the focal point for a lot of young people in the communities to have a place where they can memorialize someone without having to go to the cemetery. It's sort of like keeping these people who passed away in the neighborhood still.

Sometimes we get hired by a group of friends or neighbors. We did one wall where we painted a portrait of the guy who died and we also painted a Mercedes. He got killed by his ex-girlfriend's new boyfriend who stabbed him in a store. He was about eighteen. He was in school, and he told all his friends that after he graduated he wanted to buy himself a Mercedes. That was his dream car. So all his friends got together and hired us to paint this Mercedes for him.

For another wall—this "Shorty" wall that we did, we went to go look at the location and give them a price. Shorty passed away in '94. The wall was painted in '95 because we gave them a price and it took them a year to raise the money. And it wasn't that much. It's kind of a big wall. We wanted to do it as a favor because we heard the story of how loved this man was in the neighborhood. He would come out of his house—he was a retiree—and he would sit in front of the stoop—where we painted this actually—and he would read his newspaper. And kids would go to school and then kids would come home from school. He was like the old man in the neighborhood that everybody liked. He was always joking with everyone.

But he passed away of a heart attack. There were two grocery stores that he frequented, so they put collection cans together so people could donate a dollar, pennies, quarters. The kids in the neighborhood got together, cooperated, and helped pay for the memorial wall. The adults, the store owners, the elderly—everyone chipped in to have this memorial wall painted. And after we painted it they had a block party. So it was sort of like their way of remembering him. He's still on the stoop.

While we're out there painting a wall, it often becomes a public performance piece because people are curious on what we're doing. They walk over and ask questions. They get the information and then people walk over to them and ask, "What's this? What's going on? Who's this for?" Then, people who pass by each other every day, who have never spoken before, start these conversations. "Did you know this guy?" "Yeah, I knew him. He was from . . ." So that stuff goes on, which is kind of cool. That happens when it's done, too. If someone looks at a wall and doesn't know the person, they learn about them through the people gathered at the wall looking at it at the same time. Sometimes, when we would finish these walls, right after we were done, the people would bring out liquor, they would light candles. They have their memorial. It's done. They can celebrate the person's life, not the person dying.

For some people these become sort of like wailing walls; because after they're done—and even while we're still painting them—there have been many cases where people walk up to these walls, these portraits, and they start talking as if the person was still alive. "*Yo, I miss you!*" People use the walls in different ways. People go there, they pray, they light candles, they look for guidance from the deceased—sort of like visiting a grave. On birthdays they have gatherings, too, and sometimes put flowers and balloons next to the wall. What some people would do at cemeteries, they do at these walls.

When you're painting a wall for a friend, there's always a sense of going through memories. While you're painting, you're thinking, "Dang, I remember this person when he did this and that." But there's a certain professionalism, a certain frame of mind you have to be in, regardless of the situation, to paint a memorial wall. You have to learn to separate business from personal. We've been in situations where we've painted children's images on these walls. And there's a sad story, and it's very emotional. There's an emotional energy that goes on behind you while you're painting with your back to the crowds. There's this crying going on there, a sense of sadness, of loss.

I'm gonna tell you, my partner BG made a good point once. He just said, "Listen, I don't want to paint memorial walls anymore." There were three of us that were doing it, and he was doing most of the portraits. He said, "I don't want to do them anymore. It's too sad."

Graven Images

"It's only half-true to say that I became a seeker of graves because of AIDS," writes Paul Monette. "I grew up in a town packed with graveyards, old church burial-grounds whose tilted slates have long since lost their graven names. Even then as a melancholy boy I'd sit on a stone, chin in hand, and contemplate the cosmos."

A year before he died of AIDS in 1995, Paul Monette wrote a meditation on gravesites. In his essay, Monette takes the reader on what he calls a *"National Geographic Special"* tour of gravestones of famous writers, interlacing those trips with his return to Forest Lawn to visit the graves of friends and his own future gravesite. In "3275," an extended essay named after the number of his plot in Forest Lawn, Monette tells of visiting the grave of John Keats whose inscription reads:

THIS GRAVE CONTAINS ALL THAT WAS MORTAL

OF A YOUNG ENGLISH POET,

WHO, ON HIS DEATH BED,

IN THE BITTERNESS OF HIS HEART,

AT THE MALICIOUS POWER OF HIS ENEMIES,

DESIRED THESE WORDS TO BE ENGRAVEN ON HIS TOMB
   STONE:

HERE LIES ONE

WHOSE NAME WAS WRIT IN WATER

FEB 21ST, 1821

In this essay, Monette speaks of burying his lover Roger Horwitz and watching so many of his friends die of AIDS, most of them cremated, their ashes scattered. He talks about what having a place to visit meant to him, ruminates on his own inscription, and rants about what he considers the criminal reluctance of politicians to respond to the AIDS crisis. Yet he refuses to allow them to make him feel that his "name was writ in water."

This excerpt from "3275" illustrates how gravestones are more than the words carved on a stone, and gravesites are more than places to visit. In the way he behaves at his lover's plot and his own future resting place, he shows us that graves are often sites for ritual action and for expressing inconsolable grief.

THE PERMANENT SIDE OF THE BED
—*Written by Paul Monette*

The morning after Roger died, his half-brother came bustling into my room and stirred me from my Dalmane twilight. "You've got work to do," he said, and when I frowned in confusion, added "Where's he going? You've got to pick a place." . . .

When we got to Forest Lawn, Hollywood Hills division, the only thing left in my heart beside the grief was a horror of finding myself in *The Loved One*. For this was surely the very place envisioned by Waugh—the sweep of grass like a Palm Springs golf course, no gravestones permitted, only bronze plaques in the ground. Nothing to mar the founder's vision of a Park of Death, joyous with children playing and family picnics, all the dead having gone to heaven. Anchored at one end by a white clapboard village church, or at least the Disney equivalent, and on the other by a half scale replica of the Old North Church in Boston, of course with generous parking. Dotted about the landscape were white marble statues of stupefying vulgarity, Moms and Dads and kids in frozen groups, little tykes on their knees praying. . . .

Our Comfort Counselor, Mr. Wheeler, was not quite Rod Steiger in a powdered wig, though his nails were lugubriously clean. He moved in a cloud of Aramis that stung the eyes within ten feet of him.

Real estate came first, as it always does in California. Roger's par ents and I were driven about in Mr. Wheeler's Cadillac, two miles an hour, as he pointed out each section from Heavenly Rest to Resurrection. I directed him up the winding hill to the highest plots, where the lawn verged on undeveloped chaparral. . . . Wheeler carried a big book like a survey map, the whole acreage divided into numbered plots.

They were sold in pairs, side by side. Puffing from the climb, we decided we liked where we were. A deal: Plot 3275, Spaces 1 and 2, on the hill called Revelation. Delicately, Wheeler inquired which space I wanted Roger in. I shrugged. What did it matter? Roger's mother touched my arm and said, "He wants to know which side you boys slept on in bed." Oh. As a matter of fact, it went either way, depending on who needed to be closest to the alarm clock. Let Roger have the right side shell. "Excellent," said Mr. Wheeler, circling it on his chart. Then, offhandedly, "This section used to be reserved just for Mormons, but we've opened it up."

I looked around in dismay, only now picking out the Mormon Temple engraved on several bronzes. "Hey, this isn't going to work, Mr. Wheeler. They don't want us up here."

He was shocked. "We're all one family in death," I think he said, and I let it go for the parents' sake. . . .

By week's end we had buried Roger there, and I still didn't understand that I'd bought the spot where I'd be spending most of the next year and a half.

There was no place else to go, really. Friends would call with an invitation to lunch or an extra ticket to the Philharmonic, in one ear and out the other. Not that I wasn't grateful to pass the time, but I knew where I needed to be. Usually from three to five in the afternoon, till closing time. Mostly I sat on my own grave—my permanent side of the bed now—and mostly didn't cry. Cried most of the day and night at home already, so this was my break. Seven days a week. On Saturdays I'd bring up café au lait and croissants at noon and read the paper, just as we always used to do. I'd talk out loud to Roger, reciting him poems. Or I'd lie down and fold my hands across my chest, looking up through the trees and trying to adjust to my last address.

From my perch on the hill I could see the day's funerals, straggling out of the churches . . . And I don't know if this constitutes a statistical sample, but almost nobody seemed to wear black anymore. Pastels, a lot of lilac and lavender.

I began to wonder which of the dead had died of AIDS. So I undertook a methodological survey of the whole acreage, moving row by row for the better part of a week, checking out every inscription . . . Here and there I'd find them, young men dead at thirty or thirty-five, with a stray quotation from Hamlet or Pooh. A silent scattered tribe, the first wave of the plague . . .

. . . It takes about six weeks to order the bronze and set it in place. They send you a rubbing of the first casting (a hundred bucks extra), on which I made a myriad of fussy changes. It was finished mid-February and laid in place. I came that day nearly faint with trepidation, fearing somehow the finality, the want of exactly the right word. Or perhaps I'd tried to cram too much in. And still I couldn't say whom it was meant to address, what sort of declaration to the future—as if anyone would even notice it except for an obsessive like me. But here it was, the final word on the final hill. I dropped to my knees and read it through over and over, making sure nothing was off.

ROGER DAVID HORWITZ

1941–1986

MY LITTLE FRIEND

WE SAIL TOGETHER

IF WE SAIL AT ALL

BELOVED SON AND BROTHER

THE WISEST AND JUSTEST AND BEST

The last phrase being Plato's final words on Socrates—in his prison cell, the poison having done its work, history's most compelling argument against capital punishment.

But here I'm getting it out of sequence. First came the Christmas crisis, when Forest Lawn relaxes its rule against gaudy tributes and NO ARTIFICIAL FLOWERS. Suddenly, the gravesites are decked with Christmas trees and tinsel and wreaths and even battery lights. I'd just begun to get used to the quiet of the place, even looked fondly now on the Old North Church, and here I was confronted by a Macy's load of geegaws.

I wanted to hide somewhere till Christmas was removed. As it happened, Star and Craig flew out from New York to spend the Christmas holiday with me, to get me through it. Star convinced me to take a few days with her over New Year's in New Mexico, where I had never been. "As long as we can visit Lawrence's grave," I replied, setting myself a pilgrimage. The second day we headed north of Taos, blinding sun on the snow, to Kiowa Ranch. Off the road on a rutted track, heading uphill and deep into the trees. To the modest cluster of ranch buildings, the whole of it deeded to David and Frieda Lawrence by Mabel Dodge in exchange for the auto-graphed manuscript of *Sons and Lovers*.

You must climb a steep hill to reach the chapel, but it wasn't the altitude pounding my heart. My first glimpse of it stung my eyes. Simple, more like a stuccoed shed than a church because crafted by hand. The rose window above the door is the hub of a tractor's tire; the one above the altar inside is a wagon wheel. The altar itself is painted silver, with just the letters DHL incised on the front. A few painted leaves and sunflowers by Dorothy Brett, the painter who was their boon companion, who had to put down her ear trumpet to pick up her brushes.

But it's so silent up there anyway, just the breeze through the piñon trees and my blubbering relief. I felt as if I were standing on the Everest of death. In the warped guestbook, several pilgrims had scribbled notes before their names: *fellow pagan; a worshiper of the God of free love.* Then you step out the door into the delirious vast-ness of the desert below, all ochre and streaks of purple, and, yes, the curve of the earth besides. I had managed to come to a new place where Roger and I had never been, without expiring of loneliness. And I had the peculiar feeling that Lawrence had given this view to me, sightless himself in the urn of ashes sealed in the altar.

We went back to the chapel the next day, by which time I man-aged the visit without tears. But there was something else going on now, a sudden compulsion to get back to Forest Lawn and our place—as if this whole visit were a kind of betrayal, sleeping in somebody else's bed before the funeral meats were cold. Abruptly Star and I left, and I stopped at the first pay phone to change my reservation, bringing me back to L.A. that night, which was New Year's Eve.

I raced over to Forest Lawn next morning, full-crazy by now, terrified that Roger's grave might have vanished, or else that it had lost the magic closeness it engendered—the nearest I could get to him now except in dreams. Though still laden with Christmas, the cemetery was practically deserted, everyone staying home today to watch football. I dropped to my knees at 3275, announcing that I was home again. Whimpering rather than crying, I buried a Zuni ring I'd picked up on the plaza in Santa Fe, buried it over his heart.

And then I began to keen, rocking back and forth on my haunches. I realized I was trying to match the sound of Roger's moaning when I arrived in his room at UCLA the day he died. A sound I barely understood at the time, a lament of terrible urgent sorrow calling out but without any words. The cryptococcus had swelled his brain in the night and stolen his center of speech. "Why is he doing that?" I asked the nurse, but she couldn't say. I asked for a shot to calm his agitation, then realized he could answer me by blinking his eyes when I asked him questions. I called his sister and held the phone to his ear as she talked, and he blinked and blinked.

Now ten weeks later, a stillborn year before me, I finally understand that the bleating sound on that last day was Roger calling my name. Through the pounding in his head, the blindness, and the paralysis, all his bodily functions out of control, he had somehow heard me come in. Had waited. Once I understood that, I went mad. My moaning rose to a siren pitch, and I clawed at the grass that covered him. Possessed with a fury to dig the six feet down and tear open the lid and clasp him to me, whatever was left. I don't even know what stopped me—exhaustion, I guess, the utter meaninglessness of anything anymore.

Grief *is* madness—ask anyone who's been there. They will tell you it abates with time, but that's a lie. What drowns you in the first year is a force of solitude and helplessness exactly equal in intensity to the love you had for the one who's gone. Equally passionate, equally intimate. The spaces between the stabs of pain grow longer after a while, but they're empty spaces. The clichés of condolence get you back to the office, back to your taxes and the dinner table— and for everyone else's sake, you collaborate. The road of least resistance is paved with the gravel of well-meaning friends, rather like the gravel that cremation leaves. . . .

. . . I think I've been to Revelation just three times in the last two years. . . . I don't know where the certainty went, the solidity of the ground beneath me during the first year's visits to Roger. No matter what happened I'd end up here, the compass point of my journey's end. Surcease from the pain at last. Now that seems like another pretty story, no real comfort.

Public Evidence Of a Private Memory

As a boy in San Francisco, Arlan Huang collected river stones. He was taken by their look and feel. He loved skimming them along the water and examining the veins that ran through the hard rock. He came to believe that smooth stones teach a lesson about time because they provide evidence of time passing, of water rushing over them. They show how the passage of time can create something beautiful.

When Arlan began painting, and later blowing glass, he always returned to the image of stones. "The shapes and forms are truly ingrained in my mind," he said. With a friend he employed a Swedish process for covering clear glass with blown colored glass to produce solid glass stones. "When I form these in my hand, the stones already exist in my mind. I've been with stones all my life," he told us.

When his grandfather died, Arlan conceived a project to commemorate him called "One Hundred Smooth Stones for Grandfather." Each stone was marked with a Chinese number correlating to one of his grandfather's stories, memories, or reminders of their relationship. The stories were written down and numbered in a personal ledger.

As lifelong collectors of tales, we looked forward to hearing the stories, all one hundred of them. But, to our dismay, Arlan told us that the stories are not meant for sharing.

"Can you tell us some of the stories?" we asked.

"No."

"Can you just give one example?"

"No."

"Can you show us the book where the stories are written?"

"No."

We came to realize that the project was about the relationship of public and private, about how a relationship can be defined and memorialized both in private moments, and by creating art or telling stories, which might tell only part of the story. Arlan's project serves as what he calls "public evidence of a private memory." Death and memory are private matters. We all need to balance what we want others to know and what will live on only in ourselves. Arlan's stones are, as journalist Samuel Fromartz put it, an "homage to the unspoken."

ONE HUNDRED SMOOTH STONES
FOR GRANDFATHER
—Told by Arlan Huang

Many people think I came to New York just to go to art school, but the actual reason was to find out about my grandparents. They lived in old Chinatown. I was always very special to them, although I was never quite sure why. As it turns out, I'm the number-one grandson of the number-one child. So we had a close, long-distance relationship.

When I moved here in 1969, attending Pratt Institute, I visited their apartment in Chinatown every weekend for dinner. The stories would abound—while cooking, during dinner, after dinner. So I got to know my grandparents very well.

When I first moved to the city, my grandfather was still running his American grocery store in Little Italy. He came to America in 1911 at the age of fifteen. He came through Seattle and Vancouver. The first thing his relatives did was send him to work for the canneries in Alaska. The work was so hard that he ran away and came back to Seattle. He worked in a couple of opium dens when he returned. Quite unusually, he was a Shriner, a Free Mason. A white man befriended him on the boat coming to America. He told him about this organization, and said he would get him into it when he got to America. So he was a lifelong Shriner.

A lot of Chinese at that time were sojourners—they were going to make money and go back home. My grandfather was an entrepreneur. He wanted to make money and stay here. He came to the United States with a "paper name" showing falsely that he was a relative of someone already here. For immigration purposes he used the "paper name" of Dong.

My grandfather's real family name was Wong. His first names are the Chinese equivalent of Jack Jones. In China, the family name is stated first and would be said as Wong Jack Jones. Most Chinese switch their name around when they come to the United States. My grandfather didn't. His name was Wong Jack Jones, and he kept it that way. His sons became the Jones boys.

Years later, one of Wong Jack Jones' sons, my father, fell in love with and proposed to a Chinese woman from the prominent Fong family in San Francisco's Chinatown. The family refused to allow their daughter to marry a Chinese man by the name of Jones. They insisted he return to his Chinese family name Wong, which he did, eventually changing it to the Mandarin equivalent, Huang, which is my last name.

When my grandfather came to this country, he heard there were good opportunities in Bangor, Maine. So he worked his way out there and set up a restaurant in the Biltmore Hotel. It was a Chi-Am restaurant—column A is Chinese food, column B is American food—hamburgers, roast beef, corn beef.

Then, in 1926, he returned to China to get married. It was an arranged marriage with my grandmother, who was from a village close to his in Canton Province. He brought her back to the United States, and for a while they lived in Florida, where they helped run a Chinese restaurant with their sons. But then the immigration laws loosened, and many of my grandmother's relatives began moving from China to New York. So my grandparents moved to New York's Chinatown in 1953, opening an American-style grocery store that included an Italian butcher in neighboring Little Italy.

My grandmother died in 1976, and after she died things changed. Then it was exclusive—me and my grandfather at the dinner table all the time. He would tell stories about everything—how China formed, where the Wongs came from, how far the Wongs go back, growing up in China as a child, as well as where the Japanese people came from and where the Koreans came from. Folklore, tales, myths, many different stories.

But one story that he told was actually very private. It was a life experience, a memory, that told about smooth stones, eels, and the river that ran through his village. It was a memory of his youth told in hindsight. It was a lesson. It remains the defining story of our relationship. It was a private story, and he would just tell me. It would come up every once in a while. It was directly rooted in our ethnic past; it was about being within a particular group, within a particular village, a particular time. It gave me a historical perspective on the way he grew up in China and why he came to America.

After he died, that story gave me the idea for the project I called "One Hundred Smooth Stones for Grandfather." From blown glass I developed a method for sculpting smooth glass stones. I etched a number onto each stone. The numbers are written in Chinese characters. So each stone was numbered and coded to a story my grandfather told me, or a memory of our relationship.

I have a book that is completely private that contains the stories, one to one hundred. I don't show it to anyone. The memories and the stories are private, as I think a lot of memories should be. The idea behind the smooth stones is that there are these stories and these memories of a relationship and the stones are the evidence. That is the evidence I want to give you. I don't want to give you the stories.

The culmination of the project was an installation at the Museum of Chinese in the Americas. It was an approximation of my grandfather's apartment in Chinatown, just a block or so away from where his real apartment had been. It was filled with objects from the apartment: an old telephone, a tin of butter cookies, worn dictionaries, chopsticks, a metal fan, and a wall calendar with a date, establishing a moment in time. The centerpiece was the dining room table because that's where everything happened—the cooking, the watching TV, the mahjong games. In the installation, the one hundred stones overflow from within the dining room table—evidence I provide as an artist that I have these memories, this relationship. The concept behind it is that every person has these memories, however they store them—they're present and they're valuable, and they complete your life. They keep you connected.

I see each of these glass rocks as a touchstone, a genuine touchstone of that relationship, of that whole era. There are certain people who are links. My grandfather was the elder of his family in America. He was the link to his generation. Once he died, a whole generation was gone.

All people have an innate connection to river stones. The stones are the evidence of time and of time gone by because of the erosion and because they're such aesthetically beautiful objects in any culture. So these stones are not symbols of mourning, but a celebration of life—of life that has gone by, yes—but still a celebration.

Arlan Huang's smooth stones bring us from commemorative art back to the subject of story. "Our greatest desire," writes Daniel Taylor, "greater even than the desire for happiness is that our lives mean something. This desire for meaning is the originating impulse of story."

A final tale. At memorials and shiva houses, Rabbi Eli Ruben-stein from Toronto employs a possibly apocryphal story about the famous violinist Itzhak Perlman. Perlman was playing a concert, he tells, when there was a loud pop—a string on his violin snapped. His playing came to an abrupt halt. The crowd expected the violin-ist to disappear backstage to restring his instrument. Instead, he motioned to the conductor to begin the movement again. Then, through sheer genius and determination, he proceeded to play the entire length of the piece on only three strings. The audience was stunned by his virtuoso performance. They rose in spontaneous and continuous applause.

He silenced them with one simple sentence:

"The challenge in life is to make music from what remains."

Notes

To contact the authors for speaking engagements or for other inquiries call or write City Lore, 72 East First St., New York, NY 10003, 212-529-1955 (www.citylore.org).

Dedication

The Hannah Senesh quote on the dedication page is from *Hannah Senesh: Her Life and Diary* (New York: Schocken Books, 1966, 1972).

One: Giving Shape to Sorrow

The tale of Kiságotamí is a Victorian rendition of an Indian tale, adapted from *Popular Tales and Fictions: Their Migrations and Transformations*, by W. A. Clouston, 1887. It was reissued by Singing Tree Press in 1968. Kiságotamí's realization that she was living among a community of mourners recalls a traditional comment made to Jewish mourners: "May God comfort you among the other mourners of Zion and Jerusalem." Through this statement, the mourner's personal tragedy is related to the national Jewish tragedy of the destruction of the Temple in ancient Jerusalem and the subsequent exile of Jews from this holy city. In this way, mourners are reminded that they are joined to a community of mourners that exists and perseveres despite its grief.

Erik Erikson's discussion of the life cycle appears in *Childhood and Society* (New York: W. W. Norton and Company, Inc., 1950, 1963), pp. 268–69. Robert Butler's ideas were set forth in "The Life Review: An Interpretation of Reminiscence in the Aged," published in *Psychiatry: Journal for the Study of Interpersonal Processes*, Volume 26, Number 1, February 1963. Robert Butler also discussed "life review" with Steve Zeitlin and Ilana Harlow when they met with him on January 28, 2000 in New York City at the International Longevity Center, which he directs. Elisabeth Kübler-Ross sets out her theory in detail in *On Death and Dying* (New York: Macmillan Publishing Company, Inc., 1969, 1976). The quote from Jean Paul Sartre appears in Mary Hufford, Marjorie Hunt, and Steve Zeitlin's, *The Grand Generation: Memory, Mastery, Legacy* (Washington, D.C.: Smithsonian Institution Traveling Exhibition Service and Office of Folklife Programs in association with University of Washington Press, 1987), p. 41. Our thoughts on human beings as spirit and dust who can be known through their creations are inspired by a lecture given by Professor Henry Glassie at Indiana University. He said, "You can't study Dante. He's dust. But you can study the *Divine Comedy*. You can't study me. I'm spirit. But you can study what I choose to let you know about me through the texts I put out into the world." With one exception (see below), the comments from Thomas Lynch both in this section and the next are from a personal interview conducted by Ilana Harlow on March 31, 2001.

Changing the Way We Die

Our comments about the baby boom generation were inspired by Marilyn Webb's, *The Good Death: The New American Search to Reshape the End of Life* (New York: Bantam Books, 1997). Dan Silverman was recorded at a dinner in Wellfleet, Massachusetts, on September 7, 2000. Kenneth Doka, a Lutheran minister and Professor of Gerontology, discussed disenfranchised grief on a broadcast of the public radio show *The Infinite Mind* devoted to the topic of 'Grief', hosted by Fred Goodwin which aired on March 29, 2000. He has written and edited several books on grief including *Disenfranchised Grief: Recognizing Hidden Sorrow* (Jossey-Bass, Inc., 1990). Folklorist Erika Brady's essay "The Beau Geste" appeared in *Folklife Annual*, 1987, pp. 24–33. Philippe Aríes comments on death as a technical phenomenon on pp. 88–90 of his book *Western Attitudes Toward Death: From the Middle Ages to the Present* (Baltimore and London: The Johns Hopkins University Press, 1974). He also discusses it in his book

The Hour of Our Death (New York: Alfred A. Knopf, 1981), in a chapter titled "The Denial of Death."

Giving a Voice to Sorrow

The opening quote from Thomas Lynch is from an interview on the public radio show *The Infinite Mind* devoted to the topic of "Grief", hosted by Fred Goodwin which aired on March 29, 2000. The quote from Roger C. Schank was brought to our attention by storyteller Peninnah Schram and is from *Tell Me a Story: A New Look at Real and Artificial Memory* (New York: Scribners, 1990). Arnold L. Van Gennep's classic work is *Les Rites de Passage* (Paris: E. Nourry, 1909), *The Rites of Passage*, trans. Monika B. Vizedom and Gabrielle L. Caffee (Chicago: University of Chicago Press, 1960). Margaret Mead's concept of the "human unit of time" comes from *Blackberry Winter: My Earlier Years* (New York: William Morrow and Company, 1972), p. 311.

Sense of Place

Our comments on Benares, a city where Indians come to die, are inspired by the lecture, "Varanasi West: Environments to Die In," by Ram Dass. The lecture was part of the conference Art of Dying III: Practical Approaches to Dying, sponsored by The Open Center and Tibet House, March 24–27, 2000. The quote from Semezdin Mehmedinovic is from his volume *Sarajevo Blues* (San Francisco: City Lights Books, 1998), p. 74. The description of the whaleman's chapel for people lost at sea is in Herman Melville's *Moby Dick*, chapter 7. Toby Blum-Dobkin was interviewed by Steve Zeitlin for an earlier work, *The Grand Generation: Memory, Mastery, Legacy*, ed. Mary Hufford, Marjorie Hunt, Steve Zeitlin (Washington, D.C.: Smithsonian Institution Traveling Exhibition Service and Office of Folklife Programs in association with University of Washington Press, 1987).

The Enactment of Grief

Ilana Harlow and Steve Zeitlin interviewed Maida Owens on October 2, 1999, in Memphis, Tennessee. The story about putting one foot in front of the other to reach the land of the living was told to Steve Zeitlin by Rabbi Eli Rubenstein from Toronto, Canada, and told to *him* in Kelowna, British Columbia. The quote from Glen McDonald comes from a National Public Radio piece called "Chad's Trading Post" produced by Sean Cole.

Two: Jesse's Story

Kristen Shantz, Dennis Cunningham, and members of the Wellfleet Community were interviewed by Steve Zeitlin in Wellfleet, Massachusetts, on September 7 and 8, 2000. Dr. Rachel Naomi Remen's ritual that employs stones is described in her chapter "Making Caring Visible" in *Kitchen Table Wisdom: Stories that Heal* (New York: Riverhead Books, 1996), pp. 151–153.

Three: Storytelling

Rabbi Edward Schecter was interviewed by Steve Zeitlin in 2000 at the rabbi's home in Hastings-on-Hudson, New York.

The Dying Tell Their Story, Too

Michel Muzan's comment on dying as spiritual labor is cited in Marie de Hennezel's *Intimate Death* (New York: Alfred A Knopf 1997). It is on pages 182–199 of *From Art to Death* in a section called "The Work of Death." The comment about reminiscence being "the high road to senility" was told to actor and community activist Arthur Strimling by a health-care professional and related to Steve Zeitlin in a conversation. The comments by Barbara Myerhoff about "re-membering" are found are found in "Life History among the Elderly: Performance, Visibility and Re-membering" in *Remembered Lives: The Work of Ritual, Storytelling, and Growing Older* by Barbara Myerhoff (Ann Arbor: University of Michigan Press, 1992), edited with an introduction by Marc Kaminsky. Ron Landsman was interviewed by Steve Zeitlin as part of some preliminary research for this project in the early 1980s. The quote from Marc Kaminsky is from *The Uses of Reminiscence: New Ways of Working with Older Adults*, ed. Marc Kaminsky (New York: The Haworth Press, 1984), pp. 12–13.

The VA Troopers

"Coming Home" is from an interview with Susan Perlstein conducted by Steve Zeitlin in Brooklyn, New York, on September 11, 2000.

The Role of Hospice

"Here I Am, Here's What I Did" is from an interview with Katherine Blossom conducted by Steve Zeitlin and Ilana Harlow with Katherine Blossom at The Connecticut Hospice on October 10, 2001.

Living with Dying

The interview with Iolene Catalano was conducted by Steve Zeitlin at the AIDS Day Treatment Program in Chelsea, New York, in the fall of 1993. The comments of Cat Yellen are from Iolene's memorial service at St. Marks Church in 1994, and from an interview with Steve Zeitlin on August 21, 1995.

The Author of Myself

The famous last words are culled from the numerous volumes of last utterances at the Library of Congress. See for instance, Alfred Nevin's 1883, *How They Died* (Philadelphia: Presbyterian Board of Publication); and Walter Raimee Egbert's 1898 *Last Words of Famous Men and Women* (Norristown, Pa.: Herald Printing and Binding Rooms). The lines memorializing Karl Wallenda are inscribed on a plaque at the Ringling Brothers Museum in Sarasota, Florida.

The Storytelling Wake

Reverend Sydney Wilde Nugent was interviewed by Steve Zeitlin in the early 1980s in Washington, D.C. Kelly S. Taylor's essay "The Storytelling Wake: Performance in the Absence of Established Convention" appeared in *Southern Folklore*, 50:2, 1993, pp. 99–112. Thomas Lynch's poem "A Death" is on page 5 of his book *Skating with Heather Grace* (New York: Alfred A Knopf, 1986). That book contains many poems inspired by his experiences as an undertaker as does his book of poetry *Still Life in Milford* (New York: W. W. Norton and Company, 1998). Reflections on death are in his book of essays *The Undertaking: Life Studies from the Dismal Trade*. (New York: W. W. Norton 1997). Comments from Lynch are from Ilana Harlow's interview with him on March 31, 2001. Registered nurse Lynn Erdman's humorous story appears in Allen Klein's, *The Courage to Laugh: Humor, Hope, and Healing in the Face of Death and Dying* (New York: Penguin Putnam, 1998), pp. 29–30. Kenneth S. Goldstein was interviewed by Steve Zeitlin in the early 1980s. Kelly S. Taylor's quote appears on page 107 of her article (see above).

Death and Silence

"You Were Great" told by Amanda Dargan is from an interview conducted by Steve Zeitlin in the early 1980s.

Death on the Range
Teresa Jordan's story, "Bones," is from a chapter by the same name in her book *Riding the White Horse Home: A Western Family Album* (New York: Pantheon Books, 1993) pp. 115, 123–129.

Story as Ritual
"The Wishbone" is from an interview with Ron Landsman conducted by Steve Zeitlin in the early 1980s.

Writing It Down
Eric Miller was interviewed by Steve Zeitlin and Ilana Harlow on October 2, 1999 in Memphis, Tennessee. Wun Kuen Ng shared her story, "The Wishing Well," in Steve Zeitlin's class at Cooper Union, Collecting and Writing New York Stories, in the summer of 2000. She has continued to work on it as a creative writing student at Mills College in California.

Dreams
Writer Susan Horowitz was interviewed by Steve Zeitlin in New York City in 2000.

Coincidence as Communication
The Erving Goffman quote is from *Frame Analysis: An Essay on the Organization of Experience* (New York: Harper and Row, 1974), p. 559. Carl Jung's definition of synchronicity can be found on p. 25 of his book, *Synchronicity: An Acausal Connecting Principle* (New Brunswick: Princeton University Press, 1960, 1973). The Dominican Siamese twin story was reported by Janice Hopkins Tanne in *New York Magazine*, November 15, 1993, p. 61. Doris Ullendorff was recorded by Ilana Harlow at a casket cover weaving session at Ansche Chesed Synagogue in New York on March 19, 2000.

Judithness
The story of Judith Obodov Hardin is taken from "Dying Well: the Death of Judith Obodov Hardin," the first chapter of Marilyn Webb's *The Good Death: The New American Search to Reshape the End of Life* (New York: Bantam Books, 1997), pp. 1–27.

Michael and Margaret
Michael Walsh told his story, "I'll Send You a Sign" to Ilana Harlow, in Kilmoylan, County Waterford, Ireland, in 1992. It appears in her dissertation, *Creating Situations: Traditional Responses to the Violation of Expectations in Ireland* (Ann Arbor: University Microfilms, 1995).

Trump Cards and Rainbows
The story about Max Gimblett's aunt is related by Barbara Kirshenblatt-Gimblett in "Messages in a Bottle" in *Kulturanthropologinnen im Dialog: Ein Buch fuer undmit Ina-Maria Greverus*, edited by Anne Claire Groffmann, Beatrice Ploch, UteRitschel, and Regina Roemhild (Koenigstein/Taunus: Ulrike Helmer Verlag, 1997), pp. 233–246. Lois Wilcken was interviewed informally by Steve Zeitlin in the winter of 2000.

Homo Narrans
Barbara Myerhoff's concept of Homo Narrans appears on the final page of her volume *Number Our Days* (New York: E. P. Dutton, 1979), p. 272.

Four: Ritual and Ceremony
Although the terms *ritual* and *ceremony* are sometimes used interchangeably, ritual is used primarily to *transform* the state of things while ceremony is used to *indicate* the state of things. The insights on ritual and drama from Erving Goffman are from his book *Frame Analysis: An Essay on the Organization of Experience* (New York: Harper and Row, 1974), p. 58. Maura Spiegel and Richard Tristman's comments are from *The Grim Reader: Writings on Death, Dying, and Living On* (New York: Anchor Books, Doubleday, 1997), p. 254. Their anthology of writings about death is a good resource. Some of our comments on ritual are inspired by David Kertzer's *Ritual Politics and Power* (New Haven: Yale University Press, 1988), pp. 8–11. Doris Ullendorff was recorded by Ilana Harlow at a casket cover weaving session at Ansche Chesed Synagogue in New York on March 19, 2000. Erika Brady published her essay, *The Beau Geste* in the *Folklife Annual*, 1987. The quotes cited here appear on pages 27 and 33.

Stillborn
"We Had to Do Something for This Child" is from a telephone interview with Susan Knightly by Steve Zeitlin in 2000.

"The Feeling of Empty Hands"
"The Feeling of Empty Hands" is from a telephone conversation Ilana Harlow had with Ken Gorfinkle in April 2001.

Designing Death
Marie de Hennezel's story of Jean the dancer is on p. 156 of her book *Intimate Death* (New York: Borzoi Book, Alfred A. Knopf, 1997). Donald Heinz's remarks about the performative construction of the self through ritual can be found on p. 127 of his book *The Last Passage: Recovering a Death of Our Own* (New York: Oxford University Press, 1999). "I Know How I Want to Die" is from Ilana Harlow's recorded interview with Elena Lister in New York City, November 16, 2000.

The Last Passage
Donald Heinz's discussion of Jacob Koved is on pp. 120–121 of *The Last Passage: Recovering a Death of Our Own* (New York: Oxford University Press, 1999). The story of Jacob Koved appears in a more extended form in Barbara Myerhoff's volume *Number Our Days* (New York: E. P. Dutton, 1979), pp. 199–227. Myerhoff's work has inspired a generation of health care workers as well as anthropologists and folklorists concerned with aging.

Home Altars
We are grateful to Kay Turner for sharing with us her volume *Beautiful Necessity: The Art and Meaning of Women's Altars* (New York: Thames and Hudson, 1999), which includes a version of "House of Cards" by Marlene Lortev Terwilliger. The altar was created in 1991.

A Prom and Yearbook
Lila Zeiger's essay "If This You See, Remember Me" was written especially for this book. She writes: "Thanks to the wonderful D.T.P staff; to Tom Martin, then director of recreation, for organizing the Prom and festivities; to Bill Messina, then director of the program, for giving us the vision to

make the yearbook so inclusive; to Arthur Webb, C.E.O. of the Village Center for Care, and his executive secretary, Sharon Huston, for production assistance; and to the Dorset Colony in southern Vermont, where this article came to be."

Chronicle of a Death Foretold
Miguel Algarín's reminiscence, "Scatter My Ashes," is from the introduction to *Aloud: Voices from the Nuyorican Poets Cafe* (New York: Henry Holt and Company, 1994), pp. 3–8.

Five: Commemorative Art
Our comments on jazz funerals are adapted from *Rejoice When You Die* (Baton Rouge: Louisiana State University Press, 1998). This book of photographs by Leo Touchet is introduced by Ellis L. Marsalis, Jr. with text by Vernel Bagneris. The Guthrie Ramsey story appeared in the University of Pennsylvania *SAS Alumni Newsletter*, Spring, 1999 in an article about his book *Race Music: Post–World War II Black Musical Style from Bebop to Hip-Hop* published by University of California Press.

Creating a Place for the Dead
"Crafting a Vessel for My Father" is from a recorded interview with Peggy King-Jorde conducted by Ilana Harlow in New York City on January 9, 2001.

Art at the End of Life
Jane Cameron was recorded by Steve Zeitlin at her home in Hastings-on-Hudson, New York, September 30, 1999.

Legacies
"Drawing Father" is from an interview with C Bangs conducted by Steve Zeitlin at her home in Brooklyn on November 21, 2000.

A Weekly Memorial
"Music to Remember Him" is from a recorded interview with Marjorie Eliot conducted by Steve Zeitlin at her New York City home on September 10, 2000.

Mourning Quilts
"Portrait of a Personality" and "Sacred Fabric" are from a recorded interview with Kathleen Doyle and Sheryl Mullane-Corvi conducted by Ilana Harlow in Sheryl's home in Melrose, Massachusetts, on August 14, 2000.

A Communal Casket Cover
Sarah Jacobs comments were recorded by Ilana Harlow at a casket cover weaving session at Ansche Chesed Synagogue in New York City on March 19, 2000.

Memorial Walls
The comments about roadside shrines are made in *RIP: Memorial Wall Art*, photos by Martha Cooper and text by Joesph Sciorra (Henry Holt and Company, 1994), p. 10. "Common Everyday People Who Were Loved" is from a recorded interview with Hector "Nicer" Nazario conducted by Ilana Harlow at The Point, the South Bronx community redevelopment center that houses the headquarters of Tats Cru, on November 28, 2000.

Graven Images
Paul Monette's essay "3275" appears in a more extended form in his volume, *Last Watch of the Night* (New York: Harcourt Brace & Company, 1993), pp. 89–115.

Public Evidence of a Private Memory
"One Hundred Smooth Stones for Grandfather" is from a recorded interview with Arlan Huang conducted by Steve Zeitlin at his art studio on New York's Bowery on December 16, 2000. The quote from Samuel Fromartz is from the *Village Voice*, February 8, 1994, p. 37. The quote from Daniel Taylor is on p. 1 of *The Healing Power of Stories* (New York: Doubleday, 1996). The story about Itzhak Perlman was told to Steve Zeitlin by Rabbi Eli Rubinstein in Toronto, Canada.